D0140011

Animals of the Four Windows

Integrating
Thinking, Sensing, Feeling and Imagery

Eligio Stephen Gallegos, Ph.D.

Moon Bear Press

Animals of the Four Windows
Integrating
Thinking, Sensing, Feeling and Imagery

Printing History
First Printing . . . . . . January 1992

Parts of this book were previously published in an article entitled
Animals of the Four Windows which was published in *Voices: The Art and Science of Psychotherapy*, Volume 26, Number 1, Spring 1990. Copyright © 1990 by the American Academy of Psychotherapists.

All rights reserved
Copyright © 1991
by Eligio Stephen Gallegos, Ph.D.
This book may not be reproduced
in whole or in part
except for brief passages
for purposes of review.

Moon Bear Press
Box 15811
Santa Fe, NM 87506

Library of Congress Catalog Card Number 91-90063

ISBN: 0-944164-40-4

for my daughter, Nikaya,
in hopes that her journey
will be joyful,
creative,
and
whole

TABLE OF CONTENTS

Foreword

This is an important book. When you have finished reading it, you may find that you are questioning your previous approach to self-understanding, wanting to try out Steve Gallegos' way of looking at our functioning.

You will find yourself looking out of four windows — invited to do so by Steve. "Ah," you say, "the four functions!" Right, but there are modifications, and there is a different encounter with these functions and with it a more profound understanding. And there are always sacred animals for Steve, so, where there is a window with a 'function' there is — of course — also an animal, if we invite it to show up.

Animals may appear spontaneously also. Then it is time to engage in dialogue, listen to what these sacred animals (our 'higher nature') have said to us. Steve shows us how effective this can be. I saw one of my clients just after having read the manuscript. By way of synchronicity she expressed her feelings of the moment in the following way: "There is a caged bird, flapping its wings against the bars of the cage." I did not say: what does a bird mean to you, but I invited her to speak to the bird, ask the bird: is there something I can do for you? She did this with ease. The answers were unexpected, surprising. One might have thought that the bird wanted to be released, would ask her to open the cage. Instead he (it was clearly a "he" to her) wanted her to clean the cage, no wish to leave the cage. The answers seemed to be convincing, expressing a deeper truth than our conscious mind might

i

have known. The process needed to be pursued and brought unexpected revelation and a great release of tension, a liberation.

Steve Gallegos presents us here with a new approach and proof of its validity. He also gives variations to Jung's four functions, especially the function of intuition which he changes into *"imagery."* In all his work images play a major role and are highly respected and are given the power they deserve. That means, let them speak for themselves, rather than letting the mind reduce their value and significance. The outcome is a much more profound comprehension. The process is for the sake of reaching *wholeness* and with that liberation. One might say that he lets the divine in us have its say, because it is in us and manifests all the time, but we can hear it only if we listen and do not interfere with our analysing minds — we need to be "empty." To give emphasis to this approach Steve takes our use of *thinking* to task. It is not thinking itself, one of the four 'windows', but the way we turn everything into a thinking issue and lose depth, the sacred and lose our way on the road to wholeness.

One would wish that this book be widely read by educators and psychologists and used as a new and effective approach. Here is a true "revisioning" of psychology and a powerful means to understanding and respecting our depth. To reiterate: what we need to do is to listen, to watch, to trust and let what is sacred in us speak. We do have our active share in it also. The emphasis is on reaching wholeness through looking at the four windows, learning to use what we see there with the respect it deserves, observant of the fact that wholeness is achieved by the cooperation of the four functions with one another.

Let Steve tell you the rest in detail. I found that I could not help but be influenced by this profoundly respectful approach. I wager that any openminded listener cannot help but be affected by it.

And may all sentient beings reach wholeness and freedom and practice to the benefit of others.

Thank you, Steve.

Edith Wallace, M.D., Ph.D.

Santa Fe, New Mexico

October, 1991

Edith Wallace has been practicing Jungian analysis since 1951, mostly in New York and presently in Santa Fe, having worked in training in New York and with Mrs. Emma Jung and C. G. Jung in Zurich. She also was a student of J. G. Bennett in England.

Her longstanding workshops with collage are represented in *A Queen's Quest: Pilgrimage for Individuation,* published in 1990. She has often presented at the yearly conferences of Art Therapists and has taught at the Pratt Institute and also at the Jung Foundation and Jung Institute. She is on the staff of the Institute for Expressive Analysis and is editor emeritus of the *Journal for the Arts in Psychotherapy.* Her chapter on Active Imagination appears in: *Approaches to Art Therapy* edited by Judith Rubin. Her present day preoccupation is expressed in two articles: *What does the Face of the Modern Day Shaman look like?* and *It is Not Only the Face,* both published in the journal *Impressions.*

Edith is a prize winning painter.

Introduction

The great Sioux visionary Black Elk dreamed that he was taken to a vast tipi, which seemed to be "as large as the world itself." On the inside of the lodge were painted all the four legged, flying and crawling beings, and yet they were alive here in this mysterious medicine lodge, speaking to Black Elk of the deep mystery of Wakan Tanka, the Great Spirit, and of the destiny of humankind. The animals, wardens and symbols of our earthly journey, thus were revealed to the eye of the shaman as eternal presences in the divine imagination.

Is there then, we may wonder, a Noah's Ark of the mind, a zone of shapeshifting identities in which the human soul mutates into the thousand bright eyed, feathered, furred, horned, beaked and tailed forms of our pre-human ancestry? Is the zoosphere connected in some ancient and mysterious way to the psychesphere?

Joseph Campbell dedicated the first volume of his monumental *Historical Atlas of World Mythology, The Way of the Animal Powers* to this concept. The origins of the human mythic imagination, as he shows, lie in the vast reaches of prehistory: the great hunt, and our most ancient religion, that of the shamans, which celebrates the spritual potency as well as the earthly relevance of animals.

Animals of the Four Windows is Stephen Gallegos' second book, dedicated to the exploration of this same realm, but through the perspective of psychology rather than anthropology. In his first, *The Personal Totem Pole,* he described an entirely new mode of psychotherapy based on a visionary experience of his own, in which he saw the *chakra* system, the arrangement of psychic centers along the human spine, to be permeated by animal presences. His work in education and psychotherapy since has been informed by this same concept. Long after we have willfully forgotten our own beasthood, it seems, the imagery of the animate ecosystem still lies at the root of our souls.

Thus it is that many of the heroes of myth and fairy tale adventures meet a wounded animal when they first set out upon their journey. Help rendered at this stage of the adventure, says Jungian analyst Marie Louise Von Franz, is always returned, as the instinctive self remembers human loyalty and attention. Wonder tales from everywhere in the world teem with animal references: from the magic horse that bears the hero into — and away from — dangers to the dragons that guard treasures or maidens; from the ant or flea, who sees the important little details missed by everyone else; to the hawk or eagle whose gaze encompasses the big picture from on high. It is hard to avoid the conclusion that animals correspond to faculties of the human soul, of which the myth or fairy tale is the story of becoming. But Stephen Gallegos has shown us a fresh wisdom in the understanding of this old truth.

When I wrote *The Shaman's Doorway* (published in 1976), inspired by the powerful shamanic lore of traditional societies, I felt it important to envision a new type of human being, of which there were very few examples yet in existence. I wondered if the prototypes were best to be found among visionaries, artists, or psychotherapists, or perhaps a combination. Several years later, at a conference in Vermont entitled "Common Ground," I felt I had met one in Stephen Gallegos. The conference was a wonderful meeting of minds which had never entered upon each other's territories in this way before — biologists, ecologists, psychotherapists and artists. Yet all found themselves learning things of great importance from the others. In particular Stephen's system seemed to me so elegantly simple. He began, as I had proposed in my hypothetical model, with a vision, the one that he had while running, of animals arranged vertically within his own psyche.

The vision led him to try an inner dialogue; and he found that his psyche, in the form of the animals he envisioned, responded in a creative way far beyond his expectations. The dialogue deepened and enlarged his perspective, as I had speculated might happen.

But in my model the shaman must also share the vision, passing on the visionary fire to heal and vitalize his community. This Stephen Gallegos had already been doing for a few years when I met him. His already established practice as a psycotherapist had offered him an opportunity to try his method with others, perhaps a risky thing to do, the more traditionally-minded might think, but one for which he found immediate and gratifying results. People responded to his method, finding healing and regeneration to flow from it. People began to encourage him to teach workshops and seminars, and to train other therapists — all of which began to happen at a rate, startling even to himself, as if invisible helpers were at work. (It was just what Joseph Campbell said would hapen if you "follow your bliss.") Soon he was initiating many people in a new method of inner work. The method introduces the exploratory, creative shamans of today to their own inner deep ecology.

The animals capture the living quality of our inner symbolism — they move and fly and speak, they have bright eyes and damp noses. Their instincts may be our own, long atrophied and ignored, yet willing to be awakened. (Unlike the version described in the traditional Sanskrit texts of Kundalini Yoga, which fixes symbolic animals at each chakra, Gallegos' system allows a metaphoric openness — any animal may dwell in any chakra for a particular individual.) Do they offer a restoration of much that has been lost in our post-Cartesian world with its formal concepts and categories and its emphasis on the rational mode, a reconnection with our own instinctuality, initiative, independence, the "ways of the animal powers?"

In this new book Stephen Gallegos has opened his conceptual windows wider than before, to include the four human faculties also discussed by Carl Jung. Thinking, feeling and sensation are presented similarly to Jung's system, but his new twist is creatively insightful: the fourth function is *imagery*, not intuition as Jung has it. (Gallegos envisions intuition as potential to all the functions.) Deep imagery, alive with its own suchness, as are the animals, is not just to be manipulated for our own ends as in some psychological systems of guided imagery, but respected for its own inner vitality and wisdom.

It is a revitalization of the human soul from within that is the real goal of Stephen Gallegos' approach. The reader will find his prose clear and inviting — while he reveals to us a new (yet very old) way of revisioning our minds. This book is a must for those interested in self-exploration, guided imagery, and the never-ending, self-transformative work of the creative shaman.

Stephen Larsen, Ph.D.
New Paltz, New York
February, 1991

Stephen Larsen is a psychology professor and psychotherapist and is the director of The Center for Symbolic Studies, 597 Springtown Road, New Paltz, NY 12561. He is the author of *The Shaman's Doorway* (1976 and 1988), *The Mythic Imagination* (1989), and is currently working with his wife, Robin, on the authorized biography of Joseph Campbell: *A Fire in the Mind,* to be published by Doubleday in 1991.

Apologia

I must begin with an apology for the brevity of this work. I am at a vital choice point: I could work on this book for four more years to fill it out toward what I envision it to be or I could publish it now, in its present form, at what I consider to be a vital time for the direction of the world. I choose now.

Since I consider it incomplete, I must apologize for the instances in which I hint at possibilities where I would prefer to spend time filling out the vision in a richer, more inviting manner.

I apologize to the reader for my choosing cryptic expressions where I could have spent time embellishing and amplifying.

I apologize to all of those teachers and authors from whom I have drawn inspiration over the years and who are not cited in the bibliography, either through oversight or as a result of my failing memory.

And I apologize for any unintentioned misinterpretations which may hamper the positive ongoing struggle of a humanity intensely burdened with survival in todays changing and stultifying cultures.

I particularly want to apologize to the fine teachers that I and others *have* had concerning my treatment of the topic of education in this book. I talk of education as if it were limited and frozen. What I am addressing is the *institutionalized* form of education, where it has lost the human dimension and become something governed by sets of rules that exclude recognition of the individual in his or her fullness and mystery, in his or her emergent creativity. I have nothing but the greatest respect for the true teachers, those who have remained true to their humanity sometimes under the most dire circumstances.

One further word. This is a personal book. It is not an academic review of the literature, nor does it have any pretensions to being such. It is comprised primarily of personal experiences and realizations, either jotted down hurriedly during my travels or coming to me in the wee hours of the morning as I sat at my computer.

I write early. I arise anywhere from one to four A.M. and go immediately to my desk and write until something happens to break my concentration, usually my daughter waking.

My intention is to continue to fill out this book. To amplify, edit, augment, and generally enrich the contents until it has reached the richness the reader deserves. Then I will issue it as the second edition. Until that time I offer it to you with the humble apologies of a craftsman lacking time.

Preface

I was away on a trip when our baby died, suddenly and without any expectation. My wife, Kay, was with him. She had laid him down on the couch while she read the paper and twenty minutes later he was dead. I rushed back immediately and arrived 13 hours after he had died. Kay was in a frenzy, questioning what she could have done differently, planning out various scenarios in which he might not have died, thinking about steps she could have taken that might have prevented his death: " What if only.... What if I had....Why didn't I....Why did I....etc." I saw what she was doing and I said to her: "Talk to your thinking. Tell it you appreciate its efforts to try to figure this out but tell it there is nothing to figure out. Baby is dead and nothing can change that. Tell thinking that the way it can serve you best now is to support you in the experience that you need to go through, to support you in feeling fully all the feelings that are going on, and to help you grow from this event. Ask thinking if it would be willing to support you in this way." She did so and she relaxed immediately. Her thinking stopped trying to take charge. It realized its only role could be one of support and that there were other aspects of her that needed to handle this.

This was a situation in which thinking did not know what to do. The domains of life and death are not within its purview, and in such a situation it can only support the rest of one's being. Doing otherwise just makes matters worse because it keeps attention from going where it needs to go: in this case to feeling. Thinking tries to protect us from hurt but there are times when it must help us step fully into feeling the hurt that is already there.

Over the next several months we mourned the death of this little boy as fully as we could. Feelings would come in waves, particularly when we would think about different aspects of him, or when we would see some of his clothes or gifts he had been given. We always stepped fully into feeling, into deliberately feeling whatever was present, and allowed ourselves to cry and to grieve openly. We held ceremonies around his passing and created a small altar with a few of his favorite things. The altar still sits atop a book case next to my desk as I write.

He was a beautiful little boy, strong and alert, with a healthy appetite. He had been the focus of our lives and we were aware of the emptiness of his absence. I asked of the situation that it grow me as fully as it could, and I was willing to encounter directly whatever experiences I needed to so that his death, as his birth, could grow me and change me as fully as possible.

One of the things that I learned so clearly from him was that dying could be an event as beautiful as being born. The way in which he went, with such ease and grace, with no resistance and without clinging to anything of this world, was so clearly different from my own many years of wrestling with the fear of dying, of dreading and being terrified of the coming of that moment in my own journey. In fact, it was quite paradoxical. As much as I loved him and felt the pain of his departure, it felt strange to tell people about the beauty of his dying.

About four months later I was teaching an advanced class on the use of animal imagery in psychotherapy. One of the students was guiding me on an open journey. I had no idea who I would meet and I had no particular agenda. As I called out within myself and asked, "Whichever animal most needs to visit with me, would you please come forth," I immediately saw Coyote sitting atop a mesa in southern Utah. I had met Coyote the summer before on a vision quest. He had been hovering around the periphery of my power spot on the last night of my solo, and I went to sleep with the fear that during the night he would come rip my throat out with his strong teeth and jaws and I would die. The next morning, after having gone through my fear the night before, he came over and gently licked my throat. Now, as I saw him sitting atop the mesa, I asked him, "Coyote, what needs to happen here?"

He replied, "Come howl with me," and I saw that he was sitting over the grave of my little boy. I immediately burst into deep, deep crying. We both howled and grieved for a long time, then Coyote said to me, "You mourned and grieved the death of your son fully, but when he died there was a part of you that died also. This grieving was for the part of you that died."

We have inherited a culture that considers thinking as a mode of knowing as superior to all others. We find ourselves trained and conditioned to resort to thinking as the means of solving any possible challenge. When threatened we find ourselves compulsively thinking out what to do. When any concern arises we find thinking taking the foremost stance and we hold the attitude that thinking itself must come forth with a solution. Thinking barges forth without even an awareness that there are other dimensions of being that are perhaps much more competent than it is. But thinking is only acting in the manner in which it has been trained. Thinking is doing what it has been taught without stopping to assess whether or not thinking itself is the proper response in the first place.

We did not create this culture – in fact, to too great an extent it created us; but now our very lives, and the life of humanity itself, depend upon our ability to return to a place within ourselves where knowing is not distorted and where thinking is not confused with knowing; where the four primary modes of knowing can return to a natural balance. If this is not accomplished, and soon, this very earth and the human concern for the freedom of individuals that has evolved in this culture, will not survive.

The challenge is individual. We must each, personally, undertake and accomplish this rebalancing. In doing so we will each return to our own natural center, and the culture will spontaneously evolve to the place where rather than perpetuating an imbalance it will nurture wholeness.

We have each longed for this point of centered balance. It has drawn us constantly onward even though we were unsure of what, specifically, we were following. If we were ever to taste it fully we would value it above any other possible accomplishment.

The Four Modes of Knowing

We are so used to viewing knowing from within the abstractions of thought that we are initially struck with wonder when we recognize that there are actually only four modes of knowing. The surprise comes first from recognizing that there are only four, secondly from realizing that we have been highly confined in primarily *thinking about* knowing rather than seriously exploring it, and third from finally encountering the vastness and ultimate wholeness of knowing.

The four modes of knowing are: thinking, sensing, feeling, and imagery. Yes, I know. If you are a Jungian the fourth one will seem strange to you. Jung, in speaking of the four *functions of consciousness* spoke of the fourth one as intuition. But there is good reason to rename it.

Jung was in a peculiar position in that he was highly intuitive *and* his imagery was very powerful. Furthermore, his intuition, i.e., knowing things beyond the present moment and circumstance and for which there is no immediate evidence, came to him through his imagery. So it is not surprising that he didn't differentiate the two. It is clear that his life's purpose was to help Western humankind return to the window of imagery as a valid mode of knowing.

But there are other people, also highly intuitive, for whom intuition arrives through one of the other windows. My own intuitive window is that of feeling. One of the beautiful things that happened during my two year residency in

6

psychotherapy was that I would have certain feelings about my clients when we first met, I would know certain things about them without there being any word or evidence what-soever about the issue, and then this knowing would be vali-dated, sometimes months later during the course of our meet-ings. There is probably not a better setting in which one's intuition can be consistently validated over time. I also have a good friend for whom *thinking* is the intuitive window. Intuitive thoughts come readily to her about the clients she works with. And I have another friend whose intuition comes through the window of sensing. He loves the outdoors and is totally at home in the wilderness. It is true that for many people intuition does come through the window of imagery but this may be due more to the fact that we have culturally disallowed intuition while at the same time disallowing im-agery. After all, there is no course in the curriculum called "Intuition 101". We *do* have many other courses which involve schooling in a particularly specialized way of *thinking* — "Mathematics 101", for example — which specifically exclude intuition as a valid dimension.

Thinking

We did not create the culture we live in, we inherited it. This culture has laws that require us to be thoroughly trained in the mode of knowing called thinking. It is not stated as such, they call it "education", but it is structured principally around the mode of knowing which we call think-ing. If your dominant mode of knowing is something other than thinking, you won't fare as well in this training as will someone for whom thinking is the primary mode. If your dominant mode of knowing is feeling you will probably have a particularly rough time. You may find a music course, if one is offered, that will tangentially touch the place where you primarily live, but that place will never be addressed directly. If your dominant mode of knowing is imagery, you will probably become labelled a "dreamer" or "lazy", and you may find an art class (or sometimes poetry or literature, if it is taught well), in which you feel comfortable, at least until it is time to assign grades. If your dominant mode of knowing is sensing then you may fare a little better. You may find yourself involved in sports if you are physically fit, or in science if you tend more to stay inside.

And if you are particularly intuitive, be very careful. You will be asked to substantiate *how* you know certain things by showing the teacher that you can follow a logical order from not knowing to knowing, and if you just *know* the answer, especially where mathematics is concerned, you will probably at some time be accused of cheating. So it is best to just hide your intuition — if you want to survive.

This is the training you will be legally required to undergo. It has nothing to do with who you are or with your particular talents or makeup. The training will be supervised by an authority who is herself (most of the time the authority will be a woman) rigorously supervised by others who want to make sure that they are never accused of being irresponsible.

8

This training is so thorough that it will occupy the major part of each waking day for a minimum of twelve successive *years*. You may find this training highly frustrating, because it will occur at the expense of your wholeness. There will probably be no way you can articulate the loss you will feel, and you will be taught that the powerful people, your parents and teachers, who are demanding this of you are wise and are true guides who have your welfare at heart.

Overvaluing thinking is the cultural mode that we have inherited. If this training were in the appropriate utilization of thinking then there might be some justification for it, but it is not. We don't teach our children *how* to think, we spend the greatest part of their young lives teaching them *what* to think. We lay down certain specific patterns of thinking that we then force them to regurgitate upon demand. We want them to answer certain questions in specific ways, upon demand, and teach them that they are somehow incompetent if they don't do this. We don't allow them to develop their ability to quest and to question in an organic and nurturing way.

At its worst we impose a belief system that then dominates them for the rest of their lives. The belief system becomes the map by means of which they wend their way through a very short existence. The belief system purports to describe the structure of reality, of their origins and destiny and all that is available in between. The belief system becomes such a dominating activity (for it constantly has to be created in order for it to exist) that their awareness is soon prevented from flowing to those places of mystery, of wonder, of the experience of awe. The belief system becomes the basis upon which they rationalize their inhumanity to one another. The belief system becomes their argument for waging war and ravaging the earth. The belief system becomes the primary structure in their understanding who it is they are. The belief system is doubly limiting for within it is held not only the structure of who they are but also of who they are not. In constantly forcing our children to account for themselves verbally, not to describe what has happened but to justify their actions logically and, when pressed, to justify their existence, verbalization becomes the substrate upon which their identity in the community is based.

Knowing through thinking is the window in which we, as humans, spend the greatest amount of time and energy. It is the dimension of ourselves with which we most strongly identify. Within it, we pin down that which becomes a substitute for the experience of Being — our social identity. We have been trained to focus so intensely on thinking that we tend to lose sight of those other modes of knowing, the ones that do not differentiate us so keenly from one another and from our animal brethren.

If the thinking mode were *appropriately* educated, it would also contain an understanding of its own limitations. It would contain a knowing of the manner in which some people become lost in thinking, and of how thinking itself can come to block the door of discovery. It would contain a description of the real relationship between thinking, feeling, sensing, and imagery, but instead it contains great distortions of these relationships.

As a culture we have set up vast structures for pursuing the various directions into which thinking can go and for extending and perpetuating them. Thinking, through the social medium of sounds and letters (pictures of sound), has provided us with a vast interweaving of attitudes, behaviors, and maps of "reality," which structure us into a crystallized body, both collectively and individually.

We make broad judgments about cultures based on their degree of literacy (i.e., their ability to give meaning to the pictures), and require that our children spend the greatest part of the most malleable time of their lives acquiring the tools for, and practicing various patterns of, thinking. We are so focused on thinking that we regard most highly those people who are able to describe its newest dimensions.

But in focusing on the problems brought on by the overuse and misuse of thinking I don't want to lose perspective on its remarkable value. It has provided us with the ability to approximate and speculate about the vast extensions of time that both precede and follow this present moment, something seemingly unavailable to any creature other than the human. It allows us to look at the organization of both the very tiny and the infinitely immense, the atom and the universe. Through the window of thinking we can see organization and structure with a precision not available through any of the other three windows.

We have available some of the finest stories crafted

by some of the best story tellers that we know to have existed. This vast and highly valued literature provides us with a sense of relationship to people we have never known and to events we have never experienced.

And ultimately, it is thinking that has provided us with the creation of this vast linkage which will finally allow humanity to know itself: the intricate network of telephones, radios, televisions, fax machines, movies, and computers which, within my own lifetime, have helped us become more compassionate and immediately responsive to the plight of our suffering fellow humans. But it has also helped us become more efficiently destructive.

The core of the process of thinking involves dissection, labelling, and establishing the relationship of parts to one another through comparison. As a window of knowing it is the most highly language dependent. It is therefore the only mode of knowing that is almost wholly an *acquired* mode, developed and transmitted through the ages.

The other modes of knowing have vast dimensions that are beyond description from the perspective of thinking. But as language is our social medium it is difficult for the other modes of knowing to be socially validated. All Westerners have undergone thorough training to accept thinking as the most valid way of knowing, in many cases *confusing* thinking with knowing, and accepting the other ways of knowing only in those interstices where they coincide with thinking.

Thinking is typically misused as a mode of knowing by being loaded with a continually repeated system of thoughts, i.e., by being employed to maintain a belief system. A belief system, in order to be completely valid must be true. That is, it must adequately describe the universe in process. If it describes the universe incorrectly, however, then it will clash with the other ways of knowing and will have to dominate them in order for the belief system to be maintained. The principal difficulty with our present belief system, the one based on science, is that it presumes a knowledge of two windows, feeling and imagery, which is in error. This incorrect understanding has developed from thinking *about* feeling and imagery rather than exploring them directly, and then drawing conclusions that maintain the belief system.

Perhaps the ultimate function of any belief system is to maintain an identity, a description of who it is that we think we are. This description is always less than who it is we truly are. Thus the most damaging aspect of this orientation in our belief system is its exclusion of aspects of reality that are essential for our wholeness.

Sensing

Sensing is the mode of knowing that has led to great confusion, but not because it itself is confusing: the window of sensing is a vital and essential window. Through it we know immediately and directly of the existence of the magnificent wonders of the sensed universe and their beauty. The myriad sights and sounds, tastes and smells, soft and tender touch tell us of the infinite diversity of this place to which we are born.

It is also a window upon which our survival is dependent. Without it we would not survive. The window of sensing allows us to react immediately when our lives are threatened or endangered and to maneuver toward those places where our needs can be met and our being perpetuated.

It gives us access to those dimensions that we see, hear, smell, taste and touch. It lets us know the immediate *objective* world.

Our confusion arises as the result of a peculiar conjunction of thinking with sensing: when we begin to think that the sensed universe is the universe of reality. It is only the surface of reality. Feeling and imagery let us know reality's depths.

We have come to live in a theoretical world of our own creation, where we are taught that the objective is the real and the subjective is somehow in question. Such a belief means that we value information that comes through the sensing window far more than what comes through the windows of feeling and imagery. This book is about redressing the imbalance that has occurred.

Feeling

Feeling is a world that has been little understood because we have tried to understand it rather than feel it.

I was lucky enough to have been born into an old culture that considered feeling as a mode of knowing with value at least equal to that of thinking. But I was trained in the mode of knowing through thinking by a different culture.

14

Conflict arose as the training attempted to impose upon me the view that feeling was of lesser value. So I hid my feeling as best I could but secretly continued to value it.

Feeling is a mode of knowing *energies*, especially the energies governing our own physical and emotional movements. We tend to think of feeling as only involving emotions, but emotions are just the high and low points of a continuous landscape, the points that lend themselves to articulation in words.

Feeling is a way of knowing the emotions and energies that exist in the surrounding environment and in other people. It is the dimension through which "vibes" are experienced and through which the taste and flavor of an event is grasped. It is the dimension through which an instantaneous knowing frequently happens, even though we may have no sensory evidence to substantiate such knowing. This is the dimension of *receptive* feeling.

But feeling is also the energizer of action. It is our energy as we experience it. When strong it moves us in particular directions, either toward or away from. Its movement can be stronger than our logic or our ability to think. Much of our difficulty comes from trying to align feeling with logic, because we have been schooled to venerate logic and denigrate feeling. Our challenge is to allow thinking to come back into a true relationship with feeling, rather than attempting to dominate and control it. Thinking has been trained to distrust the knowing of feeling. Numerous times I have worked with someone in therapy, who, when a strong feeling begins to arise, fights it and tries to disallow it unless they first "know" what it is about. Thinking must learn that feeling has a longer and deeper memory than it does, and that it already *knows* why it is there. Thinking can learn to trust feeling and discover the 'why' later.

If we pull away from feeling we divorce ourselves from our energy, from our aliveness, and become relatively depressed. To enter fully into feelingness is to become fully responsive. This is difficult because some of feeling is painful, and our culture teaches us to try to diminish pain, to escape from it, rather than helping us learn how to meet it fully.

But another of the reasons we have difficulty with feelings is because of the continuum. Since energy is continuous and there is never a place where it is not, feelings do not give us the firm distinction between ourselves and someone else, or between two objects, primarily because when knowing through feeling *there is no firm distinction;* it is a continuous flow. There really is a continuity between who we are and someone else. This is one way that we can know someone else instantaneously, without having a prior history with them. This, of course, is the dimension in which love occurs.

The fact that feeling verifies the continuity of all energy is also one of the principal reasons that thinking has difficulty articulating feeling. Thinking functions in terms of distinct boundaries and differentiation, defining things by separating them from what they are not. Energy, feeling, is fluid and flows together at its edges. Language cannot well fit itself to such a dimension.

16

As a culture we are essentially illiterate in the area of feeling. Because it is invisible we have great difficulty adapting our language to it, and it is characteristically only captured in metaphor, i.e., by reference to something we can sense, e.g., "mad as a raging bull." Feeling is much more subtle than thinking, and since language is the tool of thinking, we have not developed a language for depicting the finesse of feeling. And our training in thinking involves a training away from feeling. The classroom is a place where feeling is deliberately limited; if a student has an intense feeling that student is usually removed from the classroom. It is certainly not a place where we are encouraged to enter into and directly explore feeling. We have also been trained to focus on that which can be readily named and described, and this results in the indescribable being an uncomfortable dimension of awareness.

Feeling is more like an odor than an object. It has subtle nuances and cannot be seen yet has a source, though the source may not be immediately present. It wafts forth unbidden and may at times be uncomfortable, although it can also be delicious. It can hang in the air where its source has been intense, so that it lingers. It is something we don't usually speak about unless it is pleasurable. Some people are more finely attuned to it than others. And some people may seem to lose their sensitivity to it as they grow older. When it is strong it propels us either toward or away from its source. Since it is invisible we can only see its effects. It can hover in an area for a long time yet others may deny its presence. It may build to a peak before it dispels. It travels with a person or an event like a surrounding aura. We are much more relaxed in friendly than in hostile feeling conditions, more comfortable with pleasurable than with threatening occurrences of it.

Feeling transcends the usually acceptable boundaries of knowing, since it is both invisible and continuous, and as a way of knowing it characteristically becomes suppressed early in life. The parents' primary mode of knowing is thinking, since they are already members of the culture, and it is this primary interface that meets the child upon his arrival in this world. That is, the child's open mode of knowing first bumps its head against the belief system of the parents, providing the circumstances for the first necessary adaptation. And although the mother frequently keeps open a window of knowing through feeling for her children as they grow, at least for a while, it is generally not maintained by other people.

Since feeling is invisible, many people have learned or been trained to keep certain feelings hidden and to talk as if they did not exist. This is particularly true for feelings related to anger and sex but it is probably true for almost any feeling, depending on the circumstances, the person, and the culture. The young child when confronted by a person whose words don't match their feelings, becomes confused, and ultimately learns also to not speak his own feelings. And if this is a beloved parent, the child begins to doubt his or her own feelings and, out of love, to believe the parents words instead.

Thus the eye of feeling becomes partially closed. If feeling is intense we try to eliminate it rather than ask it what it is there to tell us. We *think* about it and try to "figure it out" rather than consulting the feeling directly. This is particularly true when the feeling is painful. We try to further close the eye rather than open it wider to let it help guide us.

Many of the people who come to see me for therapy have very pallid skin. Yet after an hour or two of meeting and visiting with their imagery and feelings, they return to a ruddy aliveness. Frequently what a therapist first encounters with a new client is the backlog of feeling that has not been experienced due to the closing of the feeling eye. For if we have refused a feeling, still its energy remains, packaged and bound, awaiting that time when we become mature enough to allow its flow and experience. As the eye opens the old feelings are finally fully felt, somtimes explosively, and as they are experienced and cleared out the ability to attune to feelings that originate in the present moment begins to return. When this happens we feel like we are stepping out from behind a shroud of blindness.

Imagery

Our culture has had the most difficulty with the mode of knowing through imagery. On the one hand we hold the confusing notion that knowing through imagery is valid only when it mimics sensing. It was the philosophy of John Locke that specified this orientation, the view that the only things that could be in the mind were those that had entered through the senses. Only centuries later did Carl Jung begin to aquaint us with the fact that knowing through deep imagery, what he called the "collective unconscious," already exists prior to any sensing. It is a dimension we are born with.

At this point we should make a distinction, however. Some imagery does reflect and imitate the world of sensing, particularly our visual memory of events. We think that our memories of childhood are true to the events that happened. We don't usually recognize that the picture is colored by a strong element of feeling. Also, some imagery is under the control of thinking: we are able to imagine some things upon demand. An architect can envision the structure that he will then build. This fact has led some people to feel that *all* imagery functions in this way and that there is something wrong with imagery that doesn't. They believe that those areas where imagery overlaps with sensing and thinking are the *only* valid aspects of imagery.

And then there is fantasy. Fantasy is imagery that fulfills needs whose fulfillment has been restricted within the dimension of sensing. If we cannot be close to the woman we love then we attempt to satisfy ourselves with images of her. Or, if we are starving, we will dream of food. In this case, imagery becomes the next best substitute for satisfying the unmet need.

But it is the dimension of deep imagery, also referred to as archetypal imagery or the collective unconscious, that is the most mysterious and remote from who we consider ourselves to be. This is imagery that arises spontaneously

20

when allowed. It is to be distinguished from what I call "canned imagery," imagery that can be created upon demand. Some books on imagery rely solely on the canned approach, the creation and holding of an image in the mistaken belief that in this way we create the world. Although such a use of imagery does affect certain aspects of the body, what we create is primarily our own illusion, a crystallization of our ability to perceive. Deep imagery necessitates a willingness to discover a world that is not yet known, and to allow our own dimensions to grow larger as a result of interaction with this discovered realm. Deep imagery is a dimension with its own integrity, and although we may try to control it and manipulate it the way we have learned to do with the sensed world, we must remember that it itself is fully alive, that it has its own inherent intelligence, and that it is deeply organic, touching closely those places from which our very being springs. Our attempts to control it frequently result in its withdrawal from our awareness, so that we lose sight of the fact that it even exists. Or sometimes it fights back, demanding its appropriate portion of our awareness. In any event, the time has come for us to begin to respect it and to let it begin to teach us about itself.

Deep imagery is the primary mode of knowing totalities. It emanates from the whole and refers to the whole. Knowing through imagery is the primary domain of the shaman, who recognizes imagery as foundational, preceding and transcending knowing through thinking and sensing, although definitely overlapping with those modes to some degree.

The realms covered by sensing and imagery are vastly different. Knowing through sensing is a knowing of the outer. It is concerned with adaptation and survival. Knowing through imagery is a knowing of the inner, and its concern is growth, healing, and wholeness. It is evident that without survival there could be no healing or growing. Yet our concern with survival has come to interfere with healing and growing. It is essential that we restore the balance.

Discoveries in the Realm of Imagery

In 1982, while working as a psychotherapist in a small community in Oregon, I discovered that there were animals in the chakra centers of the body. The discovery was made through a strange sequence of events that I have described in *The Personal Totem Pole*.[1]

I immediately began exploring these animals in my psychotherapy practice and found that they were capable of healing longstanding emotional injuries in the individual, and that they undertook this healing dynamically and gracefully.[2]

Furthermore, these animals validated the classical Oriental theory of the function of the various chakras whether or not the people encountering them knew anything of chakra theory, e.g., injury in a love situation would show up as an

---

[1] E. S. Gallegos. *The Personal Totem Pole: Animal Imagery, the Chakras, and Psychotherapy*, Moon Bear Press, 1987 (second edition 1990).

[2] Contact with the animals is made by first helping the clients relax and then redirecting their attention to their deep imagery. I then request that they successively focus their attention on each of the chakra areas of the body and invite an animal to come forth from each chakra. This process needs to be done with an attitude of discovery rather than of presumption. However, even when a client thinks he knows what animal might appear, more often than not a different creature shows up and insists that he is in his rightful place and needs to be allowed to remain.

injury to the heart animal, difficulties in communication appeared as restrictions in the throat animal, etc.

I also discovered that, by working with the animals directly and seeing to their nurturing and welfare, any changes that occurred in them resulted in corresponding changes in the well-being of the person. In fact, over a period of time the animals knew precisely how to bring the person back to living in the fullness of his or her potential.

The Chakras

Chakra is a Sanskrit word that literally means "wheel," but it has come to refer to an energy center in the body, essentially a wheel of moving energy, or perhaps one of the wheels that moves us through life.

There are seven primary chakra centers down the midline of the body and they are characteristically numbered from the lowest to the highest, from the perineum to the crown of the cranium.

The first chakra is located at the perineum at the base of the spine where the legs and pelvis join. Its classical function is that of providing a grounding in the earth, depicting one's relationship to the earth, ones stance or attitude toward being-in-the-world, one's sense of security.

The second chakra, located in the abdomen or belly, just below the navel, is classically concerned with emotion and passion.

The third chakra is found in the solar plexus and is the center of power, not the power of force, coercion or manipulation, but the power to act with precision in the moment. Whereas the second chakra may be analogous to the engine in a vehicle, the third would be more like the steering mechanism. Because of this some people occasionally refer to the second chakra as the power center. In truth, all the chakras are power centers, each with a specific kind of power.

The fourth chakra is located in the heart and is the energy of love and compassion.

The fifth is in the throat and its function is communication and expression.

The sixth, sometimes referred to as the "third eye," is in the forehead and is concerned with thinking and intuition, or seeing beyond the present moment.

And the seventh, also called the "crown chakra," is located at the very top of the head and is the energy of one's spirit.

These chakras are located at certain physiological points, some of which have a classical relationship to particular aspects of Western culture, e.g., the heart as the seat of love, the intestines as the locus of emotion, the throat as communication and the forehead for thinking. And of course, the crown of the head is where the halo is located in Christian religious tradition.

The animals that I discovered in the chakras provided evidence that validated the classical Hindu understanding. However, whereas one common practice concerning the spiritual development of this energy is that of raising it to the

highest level through meditation or various devotional prac-
tices, the animals made it evident that this was not to be
done at the exclusion of any of the chakras but with the full
and harmonious inclusion of them all.

Generally, other methods for exploring the chakras
provide experiences that are at best subtle, and sometimes
introduction to the chakras is static and dictatorial. In some
orientations people are instructed to *see* a particular color at
each chakra rather than being allowed to discover what color
is actually there. Another approach is to see a fixed symbolic
image. Some Hindu and Taoist texts show a specific animal
at each chakra, as if the particular animal is fixed and unchanging. The animals that I saw and have come to work
with provide immediate access to the chakras in a distinct
and powerful way. For example, in experiencing the energy
of the abdomen, it may feel like a dull indistinct ache that is
difficult to keep in focus; but when one sees a black leopard
in a cage, angry and constrained, the impact is much more
immediate and meaningful.

Or, equally important, on those occasions where there
is no sensation in one of the chakra areas, not much can be
done other than to continue to focus on the lack of sensation.
However, in going to meet the animals, one might encounter
an empty cave at that chakra location, and the other animals
might undertake a search for the missing animal, or may
have some knowledge of its whereabouts. In any case, the
animals provide a precise and interactive means of accessing
and working with these energies.

The Power of the Council

The animals appeared spontaneously to me as I was jogging. The afternoon was coming to its end and dusk was settling over the city below. As I ran down the hillside with thoughts of the day crisscrossing through my mind I suddenly saw the bear in my heart and the eagle flying in my forehead. I immediately looked in my other chakras and saw a white horse galloping along in my throat, a whale swimming deep in the sea of my belly and a rabbit jogging along at my base. The animal in my solar plexus was a deer. They all accompanied me as I jogged on home.

My first act, beyond amazement, was to ask these animals to meet together. I was surprised to find that most of them didn't know each other. They gathered together into a circle. As they looked at one another, Rabbit, my grounding animal, immediately began telling the others how small and weak he felt in their presence, how afraid he was of them because they were all large and powerful. He said he felt that he didn't belong with them and that he should leave.

As the rabbit spoke a memory came to me of a time when I was five years old. I had just started school and had been in kindergarten for several weeks. My mother was the third grade teacher and had prepared me well for school. I already knew how to count and I could read a few words. I was enjoying my competence. One day, abruptly, the teacher came over to me and said, "You're much too smart to be in here. You really should be in the first grade," whereupon she

27

took me by the arm and led me down a long hallway to the first grade classroom. The kindergarten class had consisted of a dozen children but the first grade class held thirty, all bigger and older than I. As I sat in my seat in that first grade classroom, I felt dwarfed, highly inadequate and tremendously lonely. I wanted desperately to get up and leave but I didn't dare.

I recognized that that feeling of not belonging had been with me every day of my life since then. In every classroom, through grade school, high school, college, graduate school, and postdoctoral work, I had felt that for some reason I didn't belong in the class and should leave without ever understanding why.

Then one by one each animal turned to the rabbit and told him how much it appreciated and loved him. They also assured him that he was definitely one of them, that he was an essential part of their group, and that he belonged with them. The rabbit was deeply touched by their kindness and acceptance. They all offered their support and urged the rabbit to grow to be their equal. At this he suddenly began growing larger and larger until he was a giant rabbit about ten feet tall. The other animals stood back and acknowledged his new stature. The rabbit became very still and settled, no longer afraid, and had a deep sense of belongingness.

As the rabbit was growing I experienced my own feeling of not belonging, of being small and weak, beginning to drain away. By the time the rabbit had reached his full size the old feeling was completely gone from my body. It was only then that I realized how pervasive the feeling had been.

I could now feel the rabbit's stability. He was not very active and certainly not aggressive, but he was also completely free from fear. I felt a deep appreciation for the rabbit and for the support the other animals had offered him.

I also felt a new sense of ease in myself. And I subsequently began to feel much more settled in my own life and pursuits.

The following day I began exploring the existence of chakra animals with my clients at the small therapy center where I worked. I was surprised at how readily they came forth in people who were unpracticed in imagery, and their power amazed me. They worked with ease uncovering and healing longstanding emotional issues. These animals knew much more than I did about the status of the client, and also much more than the client knew. They were humorous, compassionate and kind, and worked directly with the clients toward their health and wholeness.

That meeting with the animals changed my life and its direction. Since that time I have been involved with acquainting people with their chakra animals, helping them gather the council and enter into an appropriate relationship with the animals. I have conducted hundreds of workshops and trained numerous individuals in the use of this approach.

The animals and their circumstances are specifically reflective of the status of each particular chakra so they can be used for an immediate assessment of the major energy dimensions of the individual. Years ago I received a call from a man who had been given my name. He described his situation: he had had an intense migraine headache for the past two weeks and nothing had been able to alleviate it. I agreed to see him immediately as the situation sounded serious. When he arrived I asked him what had happened two weeks ago. He told me that his wife had left with their two children and had gone to live with her mother. He began condemning himself, saying that he knew he was at fault and should have treated her differently. After helping him relax as best he could, I had him focus on his heart and invite an animal to appear. I expected to find an animal that was horribly distraught, and I was surprised at what appeared: a deer, calmly nibbling grass in a meadow. Each animal in turn was quite calm and content until we arrived at his forehead where an octopus appeared whose arms were stretched to the limit trying to hold everything together. It was in tremendous pain. I suggested that he ask the other animals if they would be willing to come help hold things together so the octopus wouldn't have to do it all by himself. They gladly volunteered and came to where the octopus was, whereupon it suddenly let go. The man's headache disappeared immediately, in fact, he was shocked at its sudden absence. Further followup by phone over the next few weeks indicated that he was resuming his life and there had been no recurrence of the headache.

This example illustrates the fact that the locus of specific symptoms is usually easily spotted and also that it is frequently the action of the council of animals in consort that provides alleviation, healing, and growth.

I need to emphasize that the animals are far *more* than metaphoric equivalents of chakra descriptions. They are alive. They are capable of action and transformation. And their acts determine our growth and our well-being. They also become a remarkable source of inner support and wisdom that sustains us during difficult times. When we consult them they help us keep our sights focused on growth and wholeness. Our relationship with them is vital. So it behooves us to see to their welfare.

Animals of the Senses

I was subsequently led to other animals as well. There are animals for each of the senses, the eyes, ears, smell, taste and touch.

Diane Timberlake had kindly driven me to the San Francisco airport following a workshop that I had presented in Mill Valley. On the way there I had been telling her that I was fairly sure that there was an animal in each of the senses. As we sat in the airport she offered to take me to visit with my own animals of the senses. I closed my eyes and relaxed and following her guidance went to meet these animals. In each of my eyes there was an eagle and these two eagles flew in tandem at high speeds. My ears were a single rabbit, sitting quietly, listening to all that went on around him. My animal for the sense of smell was an elephant probing the world around with his trunk.

Whereas the chakras are modes of action or power, the senses are modes of reception. The animals of the senses show us the relative relationship between the different senses, their state of integration, and sometimes their historical concerns.

Obviously all of the senses were intended to work together, but it is not unusual for each eye to be a different animal, sometimes so different that they live in totally different terrains and cannot even come to a meeting place when first encountered. But sometimes when they meet they are willing to merge together and a new animal appears in their place. This is occasionally accompanied by the resolution of some old conflict in the individual.

One man with a long history of depression and self-criticism discovered that in his right ear there was not an animal but Moses,[3] handing down the commandments. He recognized Moses' voice as the voice that he constantly heard criticizing him, a voice with which he had identified for most of his life. He told Moses that he did not like the constant criticism. Moses replied that the client knew he would be better off were he to follow Moses' advice. The client acknowledged that would be the case but said he didn't like

---

[3] One of the fundamental tenets of this work is that whatever image appears is the one to which the client should relate, even though an animal may have been requested. The appearance of an image other than an animal, while working with animal imagery, is not unlike the need to use a foreign word in order to precisely convey a specific concept where no appropriate equivalent exists in the language one is speaking.

the demanding manner in which Moses advised him. At this Moses replied that he would be happy to communicate with the client in whatever manner the client wished. The client asked Moses to talk to him kindly and encouragingly. Moses agreed. The client subsequently became less demanding with himself and his depression abated.

What we learn from the sensory animals is that some early injuries may have been dealt with at the level of the senses. Traumatic or injurious situations were encapsulated at the level of the sense organ, and perception of the event was thus modified in order to protect the child. The efferent sensory system, i.e., the system of feedback from the central nervous system to the sensory organ itself, could readily accomplish such a change. This modified input is represented in the sensory animals. Developing a relationship with them allows the quickest way I know for healing the injury and realigning the sensory organ with a relatively unbiased input.

Polarity Animals

There are also animals related to naturally occurring polarities in the body: animals for the right and the left halves of the body, the front and the back halves, the top and bottom halves, and the inside and the outside. These animals sometimes characterize conflicts in the individual, and the conflicts can be resolved by working on the animals' relationship with each other.

Many other polarities have been explored, among them are animals of the masculine and the feminine, of right and wrong, good and bad, life and death, of one's identity and its opposite.

Other Animals

Other animals that have appeared or been explored are animals of various organs of the body, animals for different emotions, and animals for various concepts or activites: e.g., an animal of creativity, an animal of deadness, an animal of being. Lisa Dickson has done considerable work with an animal for the immune system. Dr. Rene Pelleya has worked with an animal of addiction and with animals for various illnesses.

One afternoon in a training group a woman expressed concern about her asthma. I asked if she would be willing to call forth within herself and ask if there were an animal for the asthma. When she did, a small, furry animal appeared. At my suggestion she asked if it would be willing to show her a picture of the events that were occurring when it first came into her life. She immediately saw herself as an infant and remembered her father and mother frequently quarreled. She saw that when she began having trouble with her breathing, her parents would stop fighting and become concerned with her well being. The furry animal told her that this had been her way of resolving the conflict between her parents and her own conflicts ever since.

She then told the furry animal that she no longer needed to assume responsibility for her parents relationship, and that she wanted to handle her own conflicts in a different way, and she asked the animal if it would be willing to leave. The animal answered that it would leave willingly, that it had no further purpose in staying, and it disappeared. To her surprise, she began to experience immediate and significant reduction in her symptoms. Six months later she reported continued improvement and noted she rarely needed to use her asthma medications.

The Four Windows

In 1986 I was asked by a small group of people who were interested in my work to provide training for them.[4] They had all previously met their chakra animals through me and had come to know the power of the animals as allies in their growing and evolution toward wholeness. I agreed to meet with them regularly.

In preparing for my first meeting with them I began looking at ways that I could talk to them about imagery and how I could differentiate it from the other ways of knowing. I began to think about how it was different from thinking, for example, and from sensing, and from feeling.

Only subsequently did I remember Jung's four functions of consciousness: thinking, feeling, sensing, and intuiting. I was curious about his naming intuition whereas I was convinced that imagery was the fourth mode of knowing, so I promptly reread Jung's *Psychological Types*. I noted that whenever Jung spoke about the *content* of the intuitive function it was imagery. For example, he says, "The primary function of

------

[4] This meeting was organized by Judy Thibeau. Other members present were Richard Allen, Belinda Berse, Meri Fox, Linda Krupp and Lindsa Vallee. They became the Boston Training Group, a group that provided me with experience that was essential in the development of a systematic and efficient means for training people in the use of animal imagery.

intuition . . . is simply to transmit images, or perceptions of relations between things, which could not be transmitted by the other functions or only in a very roundabout way."[5]

As I began thinking about these four ways that we have for knowing, I kept seeing them more and more as windows through which we know the universe and which allow us to interact with it. Each window has its own uniqueness. Each is capable of showing something that the others cannot, yet all of them are necessary if we are to have full contact with the universe and a full experience of our aliveness.

I then began wondering if there might possibly be an animal for each of these four windows. The idea intrigued me and I planned to alot some private time for exploring it on the following day.

However, the mode of knowing through imagery did not want to wait until the following day and provided me with a preview during the night.

---

[5] C. G. Jung. *Psychological Types,* Volume 6 of the Collected Works of C. G. Jung, Princeton University Press, 1921, quoted from *The Portable Jung,* Viking, 1971, p.221. Jung speaks of intuition as being "the function of unconscious perception" (Ibid, P. 220). Intuition may, in fact, derive from the interrelated functioning of all modes of knowing, analogous to the experience of depth that results from using both eyes simultaneously rather than only one eye, or each eye alternately. Intuition would then essentially be a depth of knowing that emanates from the harmony of all four modes, and as such could appear in the guise of any of them, and to a greater or lesser extent depending upon the degree of alignment.

The Dream

That night I was awakened from a deep sleep by a dream of such peculiar intensity that I arose immediately and recorded it:

Dream: night of Feb 27-28, 1987

We arrived at the top of a mountain. It was very cold. At the top we were awed by the discovery of a sabre-tooth tiger, extremely large, and of a strong mule or donkey, both frozen and mummified, apparently long ago. The tiger was on its back with the large sabre teeth sticking up in the air. The two animals seemed to have killed each other in battle, or fought to a stalemate in which they both froze.

We picked up some hefty sticks that apparently were gathered for a fire. I found a staff that was double pronged. It felt more appropriate to use it with the double-prong at the bottom.

Animals of the Four Windows

The following afternoon I retired to a room where I knew I wouldn't be disturbed. I relaxed on a couch and went in search of my animals for the four windows of knowing.

The first animal that I met was an ant, going along a relatively straight line, stopping to touch each other ant that it met, very limited and one-dimensional. I felt immediately that this was my animal for thinking. Then suddenly my eagle appeared, swooped down and ate the ant. This completely surprised me. Eagle had been the first animal ever to appear to me, out of my sixth chakra, in my forehead. I suddenly realized that the eagle is also my thinking animal. The ant was the way I had been thinking about thinking! My thinking is much more direct, clear, and powerful than I had previously realized. The eagle told me that it was he who was responsible for the success of the animal imagery work I have been doing. He told me that it is through thinking that I am able to communicate about the animals in the first place, it is through thinking that I first knew to look for the animals in the other chakras when I first met him, and it is because of thinking that I have met the others: the animals of the senses, the polarity animals, and now, ultimately, the animals for the four modes of knowing. Eagle informed me that I must learn to respect thinking more and to realize the vastness of the dimensions it can enter.

Eagle asked me to climb on his back and he took me for a ride; this was the first time I had ever flown with him. It was evident he was taking me to the other three modes of knowing, but he wouldn't tell me beforehand which particular mode we were going to meet.

We landed in a jungle and an elephant immediately appeared, charging directly toward me and trumpeting loudly. He was large and powerful, charging at me with tremendous speed. In fact, his momentum was so great that he couldn't stop when he reached me and it carried him about ten feet beyond me. The elephant kept trumpeting in anguish, as if he were in agony. I was surprised at his power. I knew this was my knowing through feeling.

Eagle urged me to become the elephant. After some

initial hesitation I agreed and merged into the elephant. I was immediately shocked to realize how much pain the elephant was in. Its entire body was filled with pain. I also realized what a powerful animal it was. I became aware of its heaviness, its solidity, the capacity of its tusks, and its relatively thick skin. While I was inside it the elephant began stomping the ground and smashing trees. Then suddenly my father appeared and the elephant picked him up and smashed him into the ground. With this it became more settled and I then realized that its front legs were hobbled. I was also aware of how invaded it had been, and that most of the damage was done to this animal during my childhood. It was an animal that could know very sensitively by means of its trunk and could also hear keenly with its large ears.

I emerged from it and unlocked and removed the hobble and salved its legs. They were worn and sore where the hobble had been. It lifted its left front leg and I saw there was a thorn in it. As I examined it more closely I realized that it wasn't a thorn but a spike that was deeply embedded. It had been deliberately driven into its foot. I extracted the spike and put some salve on the wound. The elephant lay down and I tended it fully, taking care first of its feet, then washing and scrubbing it all over, drying it and polishing its tusks and nails. It was only then that I became aware it was a female elephant, although it had been trumpeting like a bull elephant.

Then I suddenly found myself on a camel. I thought that perhaps the elephant had transformed into a camel, but

I saw the elephant was still there, lying on its side and not looking well. The camel was rather shy but very enduring. It carried me regally. It was strong and it moved with relative precision and dignity. I became aware of it as a pack animal in caravans and of how camels initially resist being loaded with their burdens. It seemed that one of its main modes of responding was resistance and withdrawal. I became aware of my own tendency to withdraw from relationships. I thought about the way I resisted my father's demands when I was a child, although outwardly conforming. I climbed down off of it and brushed it with a curry comb. The camel was a male.

The eagle suggested that the camel and the elephant merge. The elephant was initially reluctant to do so, but it eventually agreed. They merged into one another and suddenly a tiger appeared in their place.

Eagle then suggested that I become the tiger. As I merged into the tiger's body I became aware of how unified it was. Its entire body could feel exactly what was happening around it. Whereas the bodies of both the elephant and the camel seemed to be differentiated into certain specializations, the tiger on the other hand was agile, multicolored, stealthy; it could creep silently, climb trees, wait in stillness, spring powerfully. It had powerful shoulders and keen senses. It was at home in the jungle, and it was dominated by no one. It felt good. I appreciated the way in which the camel and elephant had been essential for my survival, and the tiger felt like a worthy inheritor of their abilities, adding its own quality of tremendous integration.

Eagle then flew off and returned, seemingly sweeping something before him, which felt like a herd of various animals, including sheep, antelope, and perhaps deer. They were all herd animals, mostly white, but I couldn't see them distinctly. They seemed to be beneath me in some way. I reflected on the fact that the senses really don't see themselves, one sees through them but they themselves have no image: the seeing eye does not see itself. I then began to see that what was below me was a magnificent jellyfish deep in the sea, similar to ones I had seen in the Monterey aquarium, almost transparent, beautifully illuminated against a dark background, subtle, tremendously sensitive, with a delicacy and precision of structure. I became aware that on land, on the beach, it looks like a shapeless blob, with no particular form and nothing distinctive about it. But in its own environment it is a creature of remarkable beauty. This was my animal for the mode of knowing through sensing.

Eagle then flew me to an immense dragon, my knowing through imagery. It was just emerging from having been buried in the earth. Entire villages and landscapes adhered to the surface of its body as it emerged from the earth. As it shook them off, I realized that it had carried upon itself all of everything. Imagery is the foundation. Any world we envision is carried by imagery. It precedes all. It carries all. Even knowing through sensing has little persistence, is fleeting and delicate, like the jellyfish. It is imagery that connects it all together and gives it presence and persistence. The dragon was tremendous, immensely alive. I never did see it all, as the rest of it was covered with the outer world. The dragon asked only that I respect it. I do.

I then wanted to explore the relationship between all these animals and see how they got along together, but the eagle indicated that it was not time yet for that, and it would have to be done on another occasion.

Following this visualization I became aware that a conflict that had existed within me since the age of four was suddenly no longer a dynamic in my life. When I was four I was severely whipped by my father as the result of having done something which seriously endangered my life. I had run out into a major highway and held out my arms to stop an oncoming car, as I had seen policemen do when directing traffic in cities. Although I escaped unscathed, the car did stop, the beating that my father subsequently administered had severe consequences. It filled me with an intense rage that made me fear I would do something seriously destructive. My father also demanded that from that day forward I comply without hesitation with anything he said, and this resulted in my actions being severely constricted around him or around anyone in authority. I became particularly constrained in spontaneous expression or action. These qualities were clearly evident in the intensity of the elephant's rage and the camel's hesitation. Since their merging I no longer feel this conflict in my life.

The following day I went again to meet with these

animals. Eagle (thinking) took me first to the dragon (imagery), who was emerging from the encrustation of all that he had carried on his surface. He was very alive and serpentine. I was surprised that this was the first one Eagle would take me to, and even more surprised that he then took me to the jellyfish (sensing). Jellyfish came over to Dragon. Dragon seemed intimidated by the jellyfish, at first retreating from it. Jellyfish then latched onto Dragon and eventually engulfed Dragon. Dragon felt honored, as if it had returned to its natural relationship with Jellyfish, who was now a fine, thin luminous sheath enveloping Dragon. They had become one indefinable creature. Dragon was totally at home as the core of Jellyfish and seemed to give Jellyfish some real substance.

Eagle then took me to Tiger (feeling) who was angry and acting very territorial. Tiger began to change and became a silver gorilla. The gorilla was initially stiff and restricted in its movements but after some stretching it became much more agile. Eagle landed on Gorilla's shoulder and they went to the luminous creature. Eagle suggested I enter into the luminous creature, which I did. It felt beautiful. I became aware that sensing and imagery had been my unconscious functions, and thinking and feeling were my conscious ones. I felt that some remarkably deep changes were happening in me.

Constraints and Relationships Among the Four Animals

When I first began work with the chakra animals, I discovered among many clients that one of the animals was frequently underdeveloped: the throat animal, the animal of communication. I surmised that this underdevelopment was due to the fact that in our culture we don't teach people to communicate, we teach them to withhold communication. I reflected on my own education and its demand that pure expression be limited, both in the home and in the classroom. Expression was subordinated to the "need for discipline," to speaking only when called upon by the teacher or parent, at which time the appropriate comunication was an instant response with an immediate answer. Communication was not respected as the description and expression of one's experience; in fact, experience was frequently discounted in favor of some other authority, particularly that coming from a book or an adult. The throat animal clearly depicted how our power of expression had been restricted and shaped by society, occasionally appearing as a weasel, a timid rabbit or an ugly duckling, or other animals we usually think of as having little power.

Two other consistencies were noticed as well: the solar plexus animal in women, i.e., the animal in the power chakra, was frequently constrained or underdeveloped, appearing, for example, as a duck always diving under water or a timid doe. In subsequent work with these women on their relationship with the power animal it was found that as children they had found themselves in a power struggle with the father or mother. These had been powerful children whose parents did not know how to nurture the child's power but instead were threatened by it and demanded its suppression. I don't want to imply that this circumstance was found only in women, for it has also been encountered in men but not with the same frequency as in women. As a culture we do not raise our women to develop their natural power. Frequently a child is told that it is being greedy, or aggressive, or selfish when it is expressing the expansion of its power, especially when that power is first developing.

Also, in both men and women, the belly animal, the emotional animal, was sometimes constrained: a tiger in a cage, for example. Again, the animal's condition indicated not only a lack of the full development of emotional energy but its deliberate restriction.

When I began introducing people to the animals of the four modes of knowing, I thought that I would find the imagery animal to be injured or limited, because we live in a culture that is basically ignorant of imagery, other than the forms in which it is commercialized. But I was surprised to discover that frequently the animal most injured was the animal of the thinking mode. I found in one individual it was a monster who was furious because it was being misused. In another it was a scrawny panther who had been shot; the individual was informed that her obsessions were the bullets that were still inside it. For another, a woman with a Ph.D. in English who had been a college professor, it was a sick, injured elephant chained and trapped in a tiny zoo.

Upon reflection I found the fact that the thinking animal was more frequently in a difficult situation was not really surprising. After all, we demand that our children undergo a thorough training of the thinking mode, a training that is usually based upon some theoretical framework. That is, the child's thinking is trained to conform to a belief system rather than being nurtured in its uniqueness and allowed to develop into its own inherent organic dimensions.

The imagery animal is also occasionally injured or restrained, e.g., a beautiful white horse with a chain on its hind legs, but it is not in difficulty as frequently as the thinking animal.

The Healing Quality of the Animals in Relationship

When the four animals are brought together they spontaneously begin to heal the wounds of the most injured. A feeling lamb, for example, begins to lick the thinking animal's wounds. One senses that they are deeply aware that the welfare and full functioning of each is dependent upon the individual health and good relationship of them all, as demonstrated by the following example.

One woman, a former professor with a Ph.D. in linguistics who had published extensively, found that her thinking animal was a brightly ringed coral snake who emerged from the ether, hovered in the air and postured, showing off its colors. Her feeling animal was an egret, standing on the edge of a marsh plucking tidbits from the water. Her sensing animal was a seal, and her imagery animal was a shy gopher. The following is her own description of the first meeting between these animals.

"One quiet balmy summer afternoon, meeting

for the first time, the four animals gathered on a rocky protuberance where a river meets the sea.

"Egret (feeling), a snowy-white being of expansive grace and beauty, was quite matter of fact about the meeting. She stood ankle deep in a tide pool by the rocks while she waited for everyone to gather. Every once in a while, she extended her curved, long, thin neck, quickly dipping her head into the water to retrieve something to eat. Once she stretched out her wide, embracing wings ruffling her feathers in the breeze. Even away from her normal, marshy environment, she was relaxed and comfortable.

"Seal (sensing) was stretched out in his favorite place, enjoying the sun and the heat radiating off the rocks. He lay languidly on the rocks, just warm enough to begin thinking about a swim, a thought which always raised a chuckle of pleasure in him. Food and the cool, silky smoothness of the water began intermittently beckoning to him. As these sensual urges presented themselves, he used his flippers to toss a bit of sand from the rocks onto his back, then he absently rubbed the back of his head against a nearby rock waiting patiently for the meeting to start.

"Coral Snake (thinking), a brilliant string of black and orange jewels, curled up aloofly on the highest rock, out of reach of the water. He looked down on Seal and across at Egret from what he took to be an acceptably dry, throne-like promontory. He condescendingly eyed Seal, glad of his own sleek coils and beautifully sparkling colors, for he found Seal dull looking and gross by comparison. Egret he merely ignored knowing that was the best way for him to get along with her.

"Gopher (imagery) and I arrived last, coming from the meadow where we had just been together. Gopher was riding in my pocket, so I reached into it, taking him out and set him on another dry rock, high enough so that he could look everybody in the eye. Seal sat up, clapping, entranced by the little brown being that had come with me. Always ready for a bit of fun, Seal invited Gopher to take a ride on the tip of his nose through the water. Gopher shyly smiled, shaking his head, and began to explore the sandy rock he stood on.

"Snake was surprised at the company I was keeping. He looked down his nose at Gopher, who, startled at the sight of him, got wide-eyed and looked around for a place in which to hide. Not finding one, he backed up against me quivering, as though to ask, 'What have you gotten me into?' Watching Gopher cower against me, barely standing his ground, Snake rose up, glittering disdainfully, hissing, and began to move in on him.

"All at once, Egret stretched out her neck, pinching Snake right behind the neck and, picking him up, shook him vigorously out over the water. She then dropped him back on his rock, flexed her wings in the wind, shook her head and settled down again. Snake, back on his rock, his composure shattered, looked much more like an actual coral snake and less like the glittering piece of expensive jewelry he took himself to be.

"Gopher recognized a strong ally in Egret and relaxed, settling himself a bit more solidly on the rock. He watched Egret pull a morsel from the water and lay it at his feet. Gopher sniffed at the gift, picked it up and stuffed it into a crevice he'd found earlier in the rock. It would be good later when he got hungry.

"Seal was now sitting up looking at Gopher with great interest. He clapped his flippers, chortling, reached up and put Gopher on the tip of his nose. Then he twirled him round several times and set him down. Back on the rock, Gopher dizzily sat down and laughed. Together the animals laughed with him and, deep inside, where one knows, I, all of a sudden, Knew."

This woman was much changed as a result of her experiences with her animals for the four modes of knowing, and coninues to respect them and consult them in her life.

Intuition as a Dimension in Itself

I mentioned in an earlier chapter that Jung called the imagery window the *intuitive function* because his own intuition occurred through the window of imagery, but that intuition could come through any window. This has been explored in group workshops on the animals of the four windows, by also inviting an animal of intuition to appear and asking it about its relationship to the other four. It also appeared spontaneously in the imagery of a therapist friend of mine. She writes:

As I called out for my animal of thinking a large Barred Owl flew silently into view and took me up with her into the night sky. I thought I recognized her and she said, "Yes — I am she who appeared to you last Sunday on your way home from the Bridging Ceremony." She can see into the darkness and into the dark — and, her hearing is another form of vision. She has no need to announce herself before her arrival . . .

She says her name is Minerva, which makes me laugh. And it is *wonderful* to fly with her. She says we must go to meet with my Fierce Bird of Intuition, and she simultaneously takes me there.

He flies high over the desert —hawk-like — Eagle-like — some kind of fierce raptor — and his keen eyes miss *nothing*. He is of the Sun — the bright day, and she is of the darkest night. She says there has always been a beautiful connection between them and both are proud of me for being willing to acknowledge that — but that now it is time for them to merge.

I begin to feel a momentary pang at losing the

two of them (I have only known him for moments) — but before I can even begin to think of protesting, they fly toward each other at high speed on a path aimed directly at the other's heart. There is a tremendous impact and collision of light and out of it an enormous snowy owl spirals slowly up on huge silent white wings. She says her name is Truth, and she takes me in immediately — flying me — so that my eyes look out through hers, and my ears hear the silent gasp of the air as my powerful wings glide through it.

She flies me back to the redwood ringed glade, where Shining Heart, Coyote, and the Jays[6] stand watch by my body. She still has my spirit in her. She speaks to them from a branch high in one of the trees, saying, "This woman has known for a long time that her intuition comes through her thinking: it is time now to end any separation between the two. Thinkng and intuition live together now — they live in me, and I am Truth.

She blows my spirit gently back down into my body, and Shining Heart embraces me — calling me, "Daughter —my true daughter — my daughter in Truth." I feel *open* — wide — receptive, and Shining

---

[6] Shining Heart is an old Indian woman who appeared during previous imagery work, Coyote is an animal of Being, and the Blue Jays had appeared spontaneously as my friend was on a medicine walk in preparation for a vision quest.

Heart takes me to that place of no boundaries — that place I call home — where every atom of my being vibrates to the interconnection between all beings.

We return to the glade and invite the animal of feeling to be present with us.

A very large iridescent blue butterfly lands on my belly — her velvety furred antennae vibrating gently and her wings opening and closing. She takes me inside herself so I can experience her extraordinary sensitivity. She is so strong — she can fly thousands of miles, from steamy sea-level jungles to high snow-capped mountains — yet, she is fine-tuned to the most delicate nuances of feeling.

She says she is here to fine-tune me — that she recognizes my work in feeling the *big* feelings, and in making myself big enough to contain difficult feelings for my clients until they are big enough to do that for themselves. But now it is time to let those shimmery flashes of exquisite joy that bubble up in me shine out to the world. She says, "Let me show you what your joy looks like to the world." And suddenly the trees around us are wreathed with shimmering masses of blue butterflies — smaller versions of herself — pulsating with life and sparkling like jewels. "Would you keep that beauty from the world?" she asks. She reminds me of two different times when I did withold my joy out of some unconscious fear and shows me how that deadens me to the world.

She says, "Don't do that anymore; let your joy shine out and acknowledge it for the gift it is."

When I call out to meet my animal of sensing, I find myself with my old friend, Octopus, in an aquamarine ocean — dancing in the water — feeling the water and the sunlight through the water on my skin — exquisite sensations of bodily pleasure.

I call out for my animal of imagery and the Black Panther appears. When I look into Panther I can see everything. Panther contains the entire universe.

Inner Communication

Imagery is the primary mode of knowing totalities. It emanates from the whole and refers to the whole. Feeling is a mode of knowing energies and movement, motion and emotion. It is the knowing that energizes our action and reaction. Thinking is a mode of knowing that involves dissecting, labelling, comparing, categorizing and linking parts to one another, particularly for the purpose of creating maps and stories. Sensing is a mode of knowing the environment, the outer, the external or "objective".

Communication from All Windows

Language is the main vehicle in communication and thinking is highly language dependent. As a result we have acquired the mistaken view that only thinking is appropriate as a source of verbal communication. How often have we heard children being told "think before you speak!" But as we quickly learn in working with deep imagery, such imagery also has the capacity to communicate verbally. It is usually a surprise to discover that the animals can talk to us about things that we know nothing about; or about things that we have long forgotten. And it is gratifying to recognize the deep wisdom that the animals embody, which each person carries within.

Many people upon first encountering their own deep wisdom immediately begin to doubt that they could know such things. Self-doubt is probably the most destructive act anyone has learned. This is not to say that questioning oneself may not be valuable, but the automatic and compulsive self-doubting that many people engage in is deeply destructive. Self-doubt is an act that has gone astray and lost its organic roots.

I was conducting a workshop when one of the participants reported that he had not seen or experienced any animals. As I questioned him further, he told me that he had in fact seen animals but had immediately begun to doubt their existence, claiming that he had only made them up. I asked him if he doubted often in his life, and he replied that he frequently did. I asked if he would talk to doubt directly and invite it to appear as an image. When he did it appeared immeditely as a teacher, towering over him and dressed in a black cloak. As I helped him dialogue with this teacher it told him that it was concerned with him "getting it right". I asked if he would be willing to tell this teacher that he was no longer in school and that now his main concern was not with "getting it right" but with growing. The teacher upon hearing this became a bit smaller. I then suggested he ask what the teacher really needed from him. The teacher replied that he only wanted to be loved. As this "teacher" was held and loved he became a small child, crying. At this the participant himself began to sob deeply. When I next asked him if he would look in his heart to see if an animal were there he immediately saw a swarm of butterflies.

The origin of self-doubt may be in questioning the

conclusion that thinking has come to. Obviously, thinking is capable of arriving at different results given different inputs, and doubt in this case may be a means of opening up to greater awareness, essentially creating an opening for more input. Or perhaps it could also be a questioning as to which window the information is coming through. As we have seen, the window of thinking is different from the window of feeling, the window of imagery is different from the window of sensing. And as I have said earlier and will elaborate on again, we have been thoroughly trained to house ourselves in the window of thinking, and one of the basic functions of this mode is to discriminate between things. Perhaps the origin of self-doubt is in making comparisons, only here it has become a consuming obsession directed against oneself. But perhaps the most particular function of self-doubt is the attempt to fit oneself and ones experiences into a map, a map that thinking is busy creating and maintaining.

Coming into Wholeness

Coming into our wholeness requires that we develop communication and communion with all aspects of who we are. Only then can there be a whole that is fluid and coordinated. It is our responsibility to initiate such communication. As we grow we will perhaps remember and recognize past instances of other parts of ourselves trying to communicate with us, and of our doubting and judging minds closing the doors to such communication. Now we have the opportunity to initiate the communication and to begin to open doors that have been closed.

Any injury involves a separation. In a broken arm, for example, two portions of bone are separated. For healing to take place, the two parts must be rejoined. One of the most significant actions one could take at this point would be to assume responsibility for the general rejoining of all dimensions of ourselves, and we can do so by issuing a general call. "I invite all lost or distanced or rejected aspects of who I am to return to participate once again in the totality of my being. I apologize if I have been responsible for your rejection. I wish to learn how we can come back into our appropriate relationship and live together harmoniously. I am willing to listen to you and to learn from you now, even if I may have seemed unwilling to hear you in the past. I am on a journey of growing into wholeness, and you are essential for the success of that journey. I am asking for your help. Would you please return to me?"

The greatest injury in our being is the separation between the dimensions of thinking and sensing on the one hand and feeling and imagery on the other. This is not a simple injury; a great wedge has been driven in, a great chasm has been created. As I have tried to show, this injury is culturally created and perpetuated in each of us. The beginning of any healing is for us to welcome back the large dimensions of feeling and imagery in general, and we can do so by being willing to step directly into feeling, and by being willing to go to visit with imagery on its own terms.

Seldom have we been willing to take the first step in

our healing. When an animal appears in a dream or spontaneously in our imagery, for example, we typically just stand there thinking, "Gosh, I wonder what that means?" We would not do that with someone who knocks at our front door. Picture this: you are in your kitchen and you hear a knock at the door. You open it to see a neighbor standing there. Would you look at the neighbor standing there and think, "Gosh, I wonder what that means?" and then close the door and go about your business? Why do we think that the animal is no less insulted than the neighbor would be?

The Control of Imagery through Thinking

We must recognize that the very attitudes we have learned to hold may themselves be the door-closers. For example, one of the ways that mental imagery is currently being employed is as a means of controlling body states, e.g., reducing blood pressure or healing infection. For all of its good intentions, this is control from thinking and is like using the telephone as a one-way communicator, dictating but not being willing to listen. The beauty of deep imagery is that it allows a two-way communication to occur between us and our energies, between us and the body, between us and imagery or ultimately between us and the universe, and thus a relationship can develop. To attempt to control imagery with thinking is tantamount to teaching Picasso to paint by numbers! If we are going to dictate to our imagery or to our body, shouldn't we also be willing to listen to it and thus have two-way communication?

Many of the current "New Age" approaches to healing and growth are hodgepodges of techniques that still treat feeling and imagery as if they are mechanical objects, merely passive dimensions of who we are that can be exploited, manipulated, changed at will if one has the appropriate technique and where the "therapist" feels free to intrude and control another human being. It is important to recognize that in such an approach the locus of control is in thinking, i.e., thinking is considered to be the appropriate source for the directions given to growing. In many circumstances just changing a word is felt to be an adequate approach, that is to say, thinking feels that a slight modification of itself constitutes growth. Thinking's view is frequently biased in favor of itself.

Occasionally when I have worked with someone in front of a group and am talking to that person about my experience of them, someone from the audience will comment "Oh, that was a nice reframe," not realizing at all that I am not reframing a thing, that the place from which I am speaking has an inherent wholeness and that my comments come from an experience that is total in nature. The comments of Mel Bucholtz come to mind when, after visiting with a group of young people who were professing to become therapists he said, "These people don't realize that what I do comes not from a series of techniques that I have learned but from a way that I have grown."

Any entry into true wholeness comes from arriving at a place where all dimensions of who one is are fully respected and therefore can be free to contribute in their fullest capacity to who we are. If one part of us constantly treats another part as if it is lesser, as if it is a servant, or even worse, as if it is only a mechanical component unworthy of any respect, we will continue to be unbalanced and lopsided.

The most difficult people to work with are those who carry the belief that they are completely correct already. In them nothing penetrates. When I speak with them they begin answering me before I am through speaking. They hear me with their thoughts, not with their being. Their belief system meets what I am saying and immediately evaluates how what I am saying fits in. Their contention begins immediately. Even if they agree with me it is only because what I say fits a belief system already formed. They still have not let it into their experience. One can see this immediately in the fact that they *have* to reply, they *have* to make some comment to insure me that they know what I am saying. They are not aware that their body itself communicates, no words are necessary. And the body is characteristically bleached and clay-like, with no radiance, no spontaneity. The body for them is also treated as if it were a mechanical robot. Their search is a search for the right answer, so everything must be put into words. Words dominate as if they have some inherent meaning that needs no referent, as if they are complete in themselves, so the focus is always on finding the right answer. This kind of blindness is difficult to work with and typically only a crisis will shatter the tough verbal framework which has become the substitute for a life. And this is touchy because they might then adhere even more firmly to the verbal, becoming completely dissociated even from sensing.

I recently saw a young woman who suddenly stopped in the middle of introducing herself in a small group. She then explained to us what she had done. "This is a new technique that I have recently learned. A part of me that is my forlorn little girl came up. I am very uncomfortable with her so whenever she becomes present I freeze her in a spot and put myself at some distance. Then I call on strength, gather it, and bring it into her." I was appalled. This woman had learned to treat her imagery and her feeling as if they were mechanical events that could be freely manipulated. Furthermore she had been taught this as valid in *healing*. Her thinking had been taught that it was okay to direct other aspects of her being as if they were not alive, as if they were disconnectred components of herself. With treatment like this they were certain to remain disconnected. Later when we went to visit the chakra animals, her imagery presented itself as a series of disjointed parts. I was not surprised because this is what she had been doing to herself, but I was horrified, as horrified as if she had been hacking away at herself with a knife.

Humpty Dumpty sat on a wall.
Humpty Dumpty had a great fall.
All the King's horses and all the King's men
Could not put Humpty Dumpty together again.

This old rhyme is quite intriguing and we may think that it means that something that is taken apart cannot be put together again, but it is deeper than that. Its true meaning is that control by hierarchical authority cannot return one to wholeness. Thinking constructs hierarchies, designates kingship, and gathers armies. These are good at destruction and at maintaining rigid organization, but they know nothing of wholeness. Return to wholeness is within the domain of imagery, not of thinking. We cannot dictate the form that imagery should take in order to accomplish growth or healing, we must trust that imagery itself knows. What thinking *can* do is to support and nurture imagery, learn from it, and be willing to enter into a relationship with it.

Relationship and Ownership

Who we are is relationship, but we have constructed a mistaken self out of ownership. That is why ownership has taken such a dominant role in our social world. We can see it particuarly in the original encounter between the Europeans and the Native Americans, which was a devastating meeting between a culture based in ownership and culture based in relationship. Frederick Turner provides the most cogent account of this sad meeting.[7]

We have wanted to own who we are and everything around us but it has been at the price of disowning aspects

---

[7] Frederick Turner. *Beyond Geography: The Western Spirit Against the Wilderness*, Rutgers University Press, 1983.

of ourselves whose acknowledgment and rightful relationship is essential for our wholeness. The accumulation of conceptual qualitites that we seek to possess merges imperceptibly into the accumulation of physical things, and the physical things are turning into garbage and quickly suffocating us in our own ordure. Even the "enlightened" New Age junkies are involved in "owning" their power rather than in uncovering it, letting it come into the light of day *as what it is* and learning to live in a proper relationship with it, nurturing its growth and its inherent intelligence.

Ownership destroys aliveness by freezing us into a static attitude of control over that which we supposedly own. It becomes part of our fixed territory whether it is a wife, children, pets, or the myriad physical things that we accumulate. Did you ever wonder how the Apache could live with so few things? Even their shelter, the wickiup, was something natural that could be returned to the earth as they moved on to a new location. When we own something then who we are is tremendously dependent on it and its loss can send us into despair. When we live in relationship with something then we are always in relationship with it regardless of where it may be.

Relationship requires an aliveness, a communion and communication, a being in the moment, recognizing new qualities, discovering the feelingness in its movement, a willingness to share oneself at this moment and a willingness to listen to the other, regardless of whether the other is animate or inanimate.

Ownership divides into master and slave, relationship is the path back to wholeness. Thus, the only appropriate stance in returning to our wholeness is one of being willing to be in relationship with the myriad dimensions of ourselves, rather than feeling that we are the owners of those dimensions.

Thinking and Maps of Reality

One of the major functions of our thinking is to ferret out and describe the patterns that are encountered in our experience. These are then used as maps of reality, which we employ to guide ourselves through life. They are also what we pass on to our young as valuable terrains to know about in their lives. But the map is always an abstraction and not the terrain. One of the great difficulties with much of education is that it focuses on teaching students maps when what they hunger for is to know the journey itself.

The number of maps have increased explosively during this century. Unfortunately, we don't recognize that they have been drawn with limited tools and in turn the dimensions of the patterns we allow as valid have been grossly limited. Rather than describing ourselves in the ways we truly function, we have been taught to accept as valid only maps that are principally mechanical and logical. But our thinking, our brains, are fundamentally organic, and the organic is founded much more on feeling and imagery than it is on thinking. The maps we have drawn have been extensively crippled in the domain of feeling and imagery, because these two windows are not mechanical and do not function in terms of symbolic logic. We have shamelessly excluded them from serious consideration when drawing maps of the whole human being. That is why we have no model of health: health implies wholeness, this is originally where the word comes from, and wholeness requires that all parts function in harmony and that they be in communion and communication with all other parts. Any map which excludes or biases aspects of who we are is not a healthy map. A map that is drawn only through the windows of thinking and sensing cannot ultimately be a healthy map, for it distorts the map of ourselves and thus perpetuates an unwholeness (if not to say an unholiness) in who we are. Our fundamental health, wholeness, and holiness depend on the full acceptance of all parts of who we are and the drawing of a map in which the windows of imagery and feeling are also full participants, both in holding their rightful and appropriate positions within the overall map and in being employed in the map making.

One of our difficulties in relating to spirituality is that we have preformed maps of what being spiritual is and we then try to forge ourselves to fit the map. True spirituality involves coming into one's wholeness. The core of wholeness is spirit, and when you are whole you then live spontaneously from your spirit. Thus Buddhists say that every child is a Buddha for the first five years of life; their wholeness is still fundamentally intact.

But my concern is not with the exclusion of all the maps that have been drawn so far, exclusion can have no place in wholeness. Only inclusion can create a map of wholeness. Maps already accumulated need to be integrated into a larger whole, with a recognition of their limitations. We must create a map that stems from all four windows working together in harmony and in full relationship with each other, so that they can all have input. Such a true map will ultimately help guide us back into our original wholeness.

Distortion is closely related to the map drawing itself, and one of the most serious distortions concerns the origins of speech and language. As I stated at the beginning of this chapter, we have been culturally molded by the false notion that speech and language should emanate only from thinking, and this is why it is so difficult for us to bring our feeling and imagery into the process of map making. We have not endowed these dimensions with speech in the map we presently have.

This limitation has been assigned from a position of logic rather than from a position of experience. When we do, in fact, venture to ask the windows of feeling and imagery if they can speak to us, there is no hesitation. Of course they can! It is we who have been unwilling to listen to them or to inquire of them.

If we truly explore experientially we find that speech, expression, and communication are qualities with which everything is endowed. Yes, we can say with the scientist that the tree has no vocal organs and therefore cannot speak, which is a good, logical answer. But has he ever spoken to the tree and deeply listened for its response? The true function of our own vocalization is to allow things all around us to vocalize. This communication must *emanate from them* rather than be invented by thinking. When we allow communication from the deeper dimensions of feeling and imagery, we find that not only can they communicate, but they do so beautifully, profoundly and poetically.

Communication and Awareness

Once we discover that deep imagery is capable of communicating with us, and that feeling and sensing (including what is sensed) can do so as well, we become aware that one aspect of the belief system that we have been trained to carry is a denial of this capacity.

The function of communication is to make us more aware. It is true that communication can be used to make us less aware, as any propagandist or used car salesman knows. Such people communicate in a way that steers us away from an awareness of other aspects of what is going on. In fact, our repeated belief system that only thought is capable of verbal communication *is itself* such a propagandist. Once we begin to see through the propagandist, then the propaganda itself can make us more aware by enabling us to ask what it is that is not being spoken about. The secret is in how we listen.

When we say hello to our headache rather than trying to ignore it or suppress it, and ask it what message it brings, we might be quite surprised at its reply. We soon learn that the headache does know why it is there. It might say, "You're trying too hard, go do something else for a while," or "you're really angry at this person and trying not to show it," or "you've been straining your eyes, close them and rest for a while." When we follow its suggestion, not as a demand but as an experiment, we may see that it really does know what it is talking about.

Similarly, if we say hello to the tree and ask what it has to tell us, again, listening closely to the answer, we may be surprised at what it can tell us. I can hear a critic's reply, "But that's only the unconscious speaking!" We could certainly construe it that way, but we neglect the fact that the unconscious really is in touch with the tree in a way that we are not, so why not listen?

Along these same lines, Jung considered that health came from merely making the unconscious content conscious, i.e., becoming aware of what was contained in the unconscious. It is curious that this narrow perspective has never actually been challenged. This process certainly gives the intellect the capacity to talk about elements that may have been unknown, but it does not promote true health any more than being aware that you have a neighbor next door creates community. What Jung termed the unconscious (both personal and collective) is a dynamic aspect of our functioning in this lifetime. What is required of us is that we voluntarily enter into a dynamic relationship with it, relating to it as a partner, rather than merely observing it from the window of our intellect.

When Jung says, for example,

. . . once the unconscious contents break through into consciousness, filling it with their uncanny power of conviction, the question arises of how the individual will react. Will he be overpowered by these contents? Will he credulously accept them? or will he reject them? (*I am disregarding the ideal reaction, namely critical understanding.*)[8]

Jung speaks of *annexing* aspects of the unconscious, or *adding to* the conscious; of *impiously overstepping* a barrier, of *robbing* the unconscious of its fire, or "something that was the property of the unconscious is *torn out* of its natural context and *subordinated* to the whims of the conscious mind."[9] (Italics are mine). What kind of language is this? Either impersonal or aggressive. Is "critical understanding" the ideal outcome? But what about partnership? What about the likelihood of developing a respectful relationship?

---

[8] *Portable Jung*, p.112.

[9] *Portable Jung*, p. 104.

Knowing through Imagery

In our culture the mode of knowing through imagery has been commonly relegated to fantasy and play, or art, and is frequently discredited. Dreams have been systematically reduced to aspects of our lives that have no importance, or so we are taught. Every instance of a child being scolded for daydreaming rather than "paying attention," every time a child is told that his or her experiences during the night do not "matter" because they are "only dreams," are instances of being taught to disrespect oneself. In doing this we discount a major portion of who we are. This activity that so fills our lives has been held in such disrepute that it is less than a hundred years since its rediscovery as a vital element in our being. We are only now beginning to reaccept the validity of dreaming.

Dreaming

But we are still prone to confuse dreaming and sensing. How often do we awaken in the morning with a fresh dream and immediately attempt to understand it in terms of our sensory world. Or immediately wonder what it "means." Meaning, like metaphor, is a view from the window of thinking. How many of us are willing to experientially revisit the dream and to interact with it (*not* make demands on it). Can we allow it to move us and change us? Can we ask it to help us understand it better? Dare we ask it why it has come and what it needs from us? Are we willing to ask if there is a dream guide who would be willing to come forth and take us back through the dream again, to help us learn why the dream has come and how we can be in an appropriate relationship with it?

Mythology

The current usage of the term "mythical" as meaning something untrue or confabulated indicates a complete misunderstanding of the origins and functions of myth. It stems from a rejection of the dimension from which myth originates and a complete distortion of the relationship between the windows of imagery and sensing.

The recent popularity of the works of Joseph Campbell, particularly his series of interviews with Bill Moyers, shows the hunger that we all feel to know that dimension fully. It reveals our instinctive desire to return to the place where truth and the uniqueness of the individual coincide.

One particular difficulty, which will be covered in a later chapter, is the classical portrayal of myth as ancient and collective, a perspective that seems to negate the fact of myth's origin in the individual and its relationship to one's uniqueness and immediate presence. Myth is not born from a culture but from each individual uniquely.

Magic

Our attitude toward magic is similar. What we think of as magic is actually a perception of some of the functions of deep imagery, misapplied to the window of sensing. Multiple simultaneous appearances, sudden appearance or disappearance, immediate transportation between distant points, the transformation of one image or animal into another, a person existing simultaneously at different ages, or in different places at the same time, the seeming non-existence of space or time — all of these are properties of deep imagery and are indicative of particular aspects of healing/growing/being viewed through the window of imagery. If we first insist on understanding them in terms of the window of sensing, we then discount them because they either frighten us or do not make logical sense when seen in that window. Let us acknowledge the window in which they rightly belong and see if we can learn from them there.

Sensing and Survival

The world that is sensed through our eyes, ears, nose, mouth, and skin is different from the world that is known through imagery, and the two knowings originally had different functions in our lives.

Sensing is vital because survival is dependent upon it. The more directly we can become aware of the environment that surrounds us the more quickly we can take action against what may be harmful. To lack this awareness puts us in the position of constantly bumping into what we are blind to. And yet, actions that develop as a result of pain or rejection tend to become automatic and thus also lack awareness. We find ourselves surrounded by a synthetic environment whose ultimate purpose is to insure our survival, yet whose very existence is itself the greatest problem. When the structures we have created to insure survival override their own purpose, then the structures themselves must be removed. We find this dilemma in the individual and we find it in our collectivity.

Education Survival

When we are born and as we grow we are surrounded by sounds. This is one of our ways of knowing the world. The sounds tell of a world that is larger than we are. We learn to imitate those sounds as a way of interacting with the world. Some of the sounds are words: phrases, descriptions, commands, but these words soon flood us and in them we ultimately drown. We learn to repeat word sounds just as readily as any other, even though their expression may be ultimately deleterious to ourselves, and we continue to repeat them in our lives just as readily as a canary sings. Most of what passes for our own thought is really the phrases and descriptions we have heard others use. In fact, this is the basis for learning by rote; we do it so readily that it is encountered as one of the most prominent training methods in education. Few people are taught to, or allowed to, think. Most are just taught to repeat.

Words which occur as commands from another first begin to divorce us from listening to our own feelings and intuition as a source of our actions in the world. When the father's command is what must be obeyed, rather than the child's instinct, then authority and language have replaced the knowing of oneself and one's own needs. It is but a minor step from this point to following the commands of the sergeant or the general, or the dictates of the dictator. We have already been separated from our soul.

In our culture most of the pittance that we spend on "education" supports thinking and sensing. Children in whom the dominant mode of knowing is feeling or imagery do not survive well in this cultural adaptation system, and those who do are lopsided. Many of the so-called "learning disorders" are not disorders at all but attempts to force a child to function with thinking as the principal mode of knowing, when his naturally dominant mode is one of the others. These would better be called "teaching disorders" rather than learning disorders.

There is no animal more dependent upon others for its initial survival than is the human being. It must be fed, clothed, cleaned, warmed, and loved when young if it is to survive. It experiences any rejection or noninclusion among human beings as a direct threat to its survival. This threat of exclusion has become the principal means of ensuring its cooperation in school. Our educational system has been founded on a survival model, where the consequences of a child's success or failure in school are the same consequences that inhere in a young animal's survival in the wilderness: pain, fear, exclusion from the group. The jungle in which we force our children to survive is of our own making, and the extreme consequences that we impose result in a rigidity of thought and behavior that is tantamount to a social straightjacket.

What is lost, what is sacrificed on this altar of survival education, is the flexibility and freedom to honor the creativity and subtle origins of one's individual being as it emerges on its growing edge. This is a loss not only to the individual but also to the culture. Why is our culture static and stultifying? Why isn't our culture warm and rich and nurturing and inviting? Why isn't our culture a beautiful emerging organic event that invites discovery and participation? It is love, warmth, and nurturing that see to a child's growth. If these were employed more in our educational system — instead of pain, fear and exclusion from the group — then children might grow joyfully into adults and the use of drugs, alcohol, and addictive activities would cease.

Addictive activites, like any compulsion, are a means of avoiding rather than of moving toward. The "brilliant" experiments which show that cocaine or heroin addiction can be readily developed in laboratory monkeys seem completely blind to the stark fact that these animals are living in barren cages and not the naturally nurturing home of Nature.

The Validity of Imagery

Imagery is older than language. It is out of imagery that much of our early language developed. Phrases that are beautifully metaphoric are not merely a playful use of language, but in fact show us the roots of language in imagery. Curiously it is imagery, and in particular animal imagery, that gave us our alphabet, through the hieroglyphs of the ancient Egyptians. Animal sounds were probably the sounds

76

we heard and made most consistently before we developed our own human sounds, so it seems only fitting that animal pictures be the first pictures of sound. Paradoxically, written language has done perhaps the most damage to imagery by providing the impression that words are concrete verities and that concepts are eternal. This idea moves us into linear time and removes us from the aliveness and immediacy of imagery.

I am sometimes asked, timidly, "Is it okay to have an imaginary animal?" as if the acceptability of the griffin or the unicorn must first be validated before one can fully accept the fact that this is what their imagery has presented. How careful we are to shield the uniqueness of our imagery from the validating public.

I have also met people who have said to me, "It is so good to find someone to whom I can speak seriously about these animals that have been coming to me all my life!"

We have long used as our standard the window of sensing, and we have been taught that imagery is somehow supposed to be subordinated to sensing. Furthermore, the sensing must be a sensing that we all agree upon, i.e., it must be commonly acknowledged. One of our major classification schemas for psychosis is that the person hears or sees something that is not there. We call this a hallucination. What it is, in fact, is imagery so powerful that it has overridden knowing through sensing. We may call this "crazy," but it is only the reverse of the overriding that we have been taught is legitimate.

Many people who are able to return to deep imagery are amazed to find that it has a life and a spontaneity of its own, that it is not prone to follow the dictates of the will, that it has a knowing which it is willing to share. A beautiful aspect of working with animal imagery is the return of humor that occurs in the person, bringing about a balance in what had become a mind that thought seriousness was the ultimate truth. Many people are amazed to find that imagery is different from thought, and that their thoughts about which images would appear turn out to be inaccurate. Not infrequently an animal appears that the person rejects and tries to drive away, but the animal holds its own, insisting that this is where it belongs. The growth of the individual emerges from developing a relationship with those deeper elements that had been rejected.

The Pendulum Swings Back

The culture that we have all inherited is a culture that has decreed that thinking and sensing be the primary focus of attention. Powerful institutions have been created to maintain this dominance. The unbalanced nature of such an orientation has finally caused the pendulum to begin to swing in the opposite direction. The strong rise of imagery and the emerging popularity of shamanism both attest to this. Our renewed interest in imagery and shamanism are organic attempts of the culture to restore the human balance. The four modes of knowing are the foundation whose health, harmony and balance need be attended to specifically. Our lives, collectively and individually, will continue to be unbalanced until all our modes of knowing are functioning at their optimum and exist in full communion with one another.

It is also evident that our modes of knowing function best when supported by one another. We need to be alert when our ways of "educating" are truly facilitating and enhancing and when they interfere with our wholeness. The best support is for the four modes of knowing to work together and for us to commit ourselves to their nurturing.

Thinking in Support of Wholeness

It is time that thinking begin to acknowledge its limits. Thinking must realize that it has been diligently trained to expect to control everything. When situations arise that are not within its natural domain, it exerts itself strenuously trying to think up what to do and how to make logical sense of the situation. A particular problem involves communicating one's indescribable experiences to another. Roger Sperry, in his classic split-brain studies, found that his patients would create fictional explanations when their speaking brain could not readily access the cause of the action.

A stunning portrayal of the conflict between thinking and imagery is the nucleus of Bergman's magnificent movie *Fanny and Alexander*, in which austere thinking, in the guise of the parson, tries to crush imagery, as portrayed by the boy Alexander. The richness and color and aliveness of Alexander's maternal home stands in stark contrast to the black and white existence of the parson, who lives strictly by rules, many of which are harsh and cruel. The parson calls Alexander's rich imagery "lies," and Alexander eventually submits to the parson's painful cruelty, knowing that it is the only way out of the situation. He is ultimately rescued by a magnificent old Jew, who uses the capacity of magic to carry Alexander away from his imprisonment by the parson.

Subsequently, living in the Jew's rich antique shop, Alexander discover's Ishmael, who is kept locked in a room. The androgynous Ishmael has the capacity to see events that are happening elsewhere — or is it the capacity to cause those events? He helps Alexander understand that this is a dimension that cannot be avoided if one is to return to to one's Original Home.

Thinking Comes Back into Balance

My own experience has been that when thinking is addressed directly and appreciatively it is more than willing, in fact it is greatly relieved, to come back into its original relationship with the other modes of knowing.

"Thinking, I feel badly about what you have been forced to go through. I deeply appreciate the fact that you have been willing to assume full responsibility for my welfare and survival. I know I have demanded that you come up with answers whenever I was in trouble. I know I have been angry at you whenever you could not provide the "correct" answers. I know I have asked you to do things that were never in your domain to know about or do in the first place.

"And you have done whatever I requested of you

with nobility and with honor. You are a valiant and worthy dimension of this being that I am beginning to discover that I am also part of. Thank you for your willingness to take all of this upon yourself.

"Now I would like to ask you to help me grow. To support my growing and to let yourself come back into a natural relationship with all the other aspects of this being of which we are both parts. Would you be willing to do so?"

And thinking replies, "You mean it wasn't my job to do all those things in the first place??? You mean I really wasn't supposed to know how to do all those things that I didn't know how to do anyway? You mean there are other aspects of this being whose job it is to do things that I haven't the foggiest notion about? Wow! What a relief! You mean I can come along for the ride and enjoy and watch and learn? You mean I can just relax a lot of the time and come onto the scene when it involves something that I'm really good at doing? Wow! That sounds good. Yes, certainly I'll be available. And how good it is to have company! Wow! What a relief!"

The Quest

Perhaps we have ignored the most common aspect of thinking, and that is the ability of thinking to question. Any parent knows that a child's discovery of the ability to ask questions is followed by relentless practice and exploration of this quality. The child becomes engrossed in exploring where questioning can go and where it cannot. And it revels in the power of questioning! The parent or other human is also deeply engaged by being questioned as by nothing else. And the interesting thing is the automatic assumption on the part of the child that every question has an answer. Thinking, at this stage, has come into its foundational organic wholeness. Rather than just labeling, thinking here gains a power it did not previously have, a dynamic dimension, a vector, a movement that conveys us on a path with profound intensity. But where does that path lead?

Thinking, in its ability to question, taps into a dynamic dimension that allows a movement toward something other than the question itself, toward an answer, we think, and we know the answer by its ability to satisfy the question and thus to bring the question to an end; the answer kills a question the way food kills hunger. But what is the nature of questioning? Is questioning itself the unification of thinking with something deeper?

A question initiates a search. A question makes us aware of an incompleteness. A question points toward something that exists, yet which we do not know. A question points toward missing knowledge. Toward a mystery which when finally encountered provides a curiously satisfying experience, the experience of a sudden wholeness. This is why murder mysteries have such a grip on people. The gap, the mssing link, the unknown, has a powerful grab on thinking, and there is a relentless movement toward filling in that void. In the murder mystery there is yet another element brought into focus. The question pursues the one who has killed life. The resolution of the murder mystery is usually the killing of the one who has killed; the removal of that one from occupying the position of being mystery.

The questioning itself is the heart, is the mystery. Questioning lives in the mystery of not knowing. The existence of questioning is dependent upon the not knowing. It is the unkown that is at the heart of the question. Without the unknown, questioning would not exist. The question is the link between the unknown and the known. The question is the place where thought emanates from the deeper organic dimensions that spawn it, seemingly in search of something in the beyond, yet what it ultimately seeks is the place that gives it origin.

Thought embodies the awareness of our coming forth, out of that deep, dark mystery. Thought embodies the awareness of our going forth, into that deep dark mystery from which we came.

The quest is always a quest toward wholeness, toward greater inclusion, toward completeness. The quest is always a move toward the inclusion of the coming forth, the emanation, the creation. The quest involves an openness toward the unknown, a knowing that our movement must be undertaken in full trust that a deeper dimension than who we are bears us forth and draws us back. The completion of the cycle. The return of the wanderer to his true home. The answer is itself the questioning.

Our Mythological Illiteracy

We have a misconstrued understanding of mythology. We have looked at it only historically. Unfortunately, the restricted view we have held too long is, "Myths are not sown like gardens; they are inherited from the past."[10]

That which we have been calling mythology so far is actually an archeology of mythology. We have spent our time digging up the mythological bones of past cultures and have failed to recognize its living presence and essential nature in each of us. We view mythology as something that emerges out of the past, like an old belief system that was held by entire cultures. What we fail to see is that mythology is potentially alive in each of us, and that the true source of mythology is something intimately personal and fundamentally essential to the fulfillment of who we are individually. Mythology grows us back into our natural relationship with the universe, but only if we honor its unique emergence in ourselves.

If some distant future culture, after having long lost the ability to read, were to discover a cache of books and began to revere the books and speculate about what they may have been about, without ever realizing that they themselves had the capacity to read, they would be in a situation

---

[10] John Bierhorst. *The Mythology of North America*, William Morrow: New York, 1985, p.1.

analogous to where we presently stand with mythology.

Experience with the animals lets us know that mythology is something brilliantly alive, in the moment, and if we will relate to it directly then our growth, our healing, and our aliveness are its concern.

The narrow dimension that we usually presume to be the foundation of our individual nature, namely, the sequence of motivated memories that we call our personal past, is in fact, the skeleton of our emotional crystallization. The individual memories are the places where our energy has become embedded in a limited number of experiences. As we work with the animals this energy is melted, the memories cease to have their particular emotional pull, and the energy is freed to return to the general energy reservoir available for being present with whatever situation arises NOW! By then, drawing an understanding of who one is from the events of one's personal past also melts into a general pool of imagery and one comes to understand much more fully that one is present now, and that the mythological dimension is a much more adequate description of the foundation of one's being than those overworked frozen memories of what once had been.

As a beautiful example of the importance of deep imagery (and thus of mythology) as a living event in one's life, I present here a few pages taken from a book being written by Margaret Vasington.[11] For the past ten years Mar-

---

[11] Margaret Vasington. *Joe's Journey: One Man's Heroic Search*

garet has volunteered one day a week doing therapy with prisoners at Connecticut Correctional Institution – Somers, a maximum security prison.

Joe, the inmate, is in his thirties, a man who as a child was constantly brutalized, rejected, and tormented. After first meeting his chakra animals with Margaret, they began visiting him spontaneously as he lay on his bunk in his cell. He had been visiting with his animals for about two years at the time the following visualization occurred.

The selection also displays the beautiful place he had come to in his relationship with his animals and the deep, mutual respect felt between them. Very minor editing, for better readability, has been done on his original writings.

I had not been able to free myself from the image of the Rose. It kept coming into my mind along with the questions: "What does it mean? and why does it seem so important for me to find out?"

I called my animals together in council and after much discussion we still had no answers. Lion suggested that the only way for me to find out what the Rose symbolized was to ask the Large Black Bird who dropped the Rose on the Island. I tried to contact this strange mysterious bird but nothing happened so I asked all the animals to concentrate with me to call him to our Island. Again, he did not appear.

Elephant said that if this strange bird would not come

---

for his Soul, (currently in preparation).

to us then we would have to go to him. We all discussed this and then it was agreed, I would go with the whale. He and I alone on a quest to find this Bird. I left, hugging each one goodbye and again I asked Lion to come but he said that for this part of my journey I must not rely on him, that I needed to rely more on myself and so I left, saddled on Whale's back.

Whale and I sailed on and on. I felt very content and was enjoying myself. The water was calm like a sheet of glass and the sun was bathing us in its warmth. Several times I drifted in and out of sleep. It was very very peaceful and pleasant.

In the distance I could hear a strange sound. A shushing sound. As we sailed further it became louder and louder. I also noticed a change in our speed. We seemed to be moving faster. The noise became louder and the wind suddenly picked up and began to push faster.

"Whale," I shouted, "what's happening?"

"Look ahead," he answered.

I was surprised to see that ahead of us in every direction was a fall. It was as if the sea ended. The only way for us to go forward would be to go over the falls. It was very strange, as if the sea I've been on changed levels. I had Whale swim us toward the edge, looking down was frightening. It looked to be a 200 foot drop. The current and the wind made it very difficult for Whale to hold our place as it was pushing toward the edge. With a sudden twist and turn of his huge powerful body Whale

pulled us away in the direction from which we had come,
into a position where we could rest and think out our next
move.

"What is this place?" I asked.

"It is the end of the water, or the beginning."

"Don't talk in riddles, Whale. You know I don't like
that."

He smiled.

"What can we do?" I asked.

"There are only two choices, either we jump the
falls and continue or return to the Island. It is the only
way."

"But if we jump the falls how can we return? You
can't climb them."

"Do not concern yourself with me. You must decide
to go forward or return to the safety of what's familiar to
you. Only you can decide, Joe. That's what Lion meant
when he said rely not on him but on yourself."

"But what if this is a mistake? What if I make the
wrong decision? What if you can't get back home?"

"What if! What if!" Whale said. Life is filled with what
if's. Have you forgotten why we are here in the first place?"

"All right, Whale, you made your point. We go," I
said.

"Hold on very tightly. I will build up as much speed
as I can and try to push us over the falls with enough
distance to clear the rocks below."

I had a flashback of a movie, Butch Cassidy and the

Sundance Kid, when they jumped from the top of a mountain into the river and as we sailed over the edge I could see and feel myself falling. We hit the water and Whale's weight brought us under and then upwards. The water had a very fast current, like rapids, and it pulled us around and out into a new ocean.

The water was calm and the sky clear. There was nothing but water and sky as far as we could see in any direction except for a dark spot just on the edge of the horizon. Up till now we had been following the Sun. Curious about what the spot was we decided to head for it, changing our course.

As we sailed, it grew larger and larger until I could see that it was a large rock sticking out of the water, perhaps the summit of an ancient mountain.

As we came closer I could see that there was some-one or something sitting on top of this rock.

It was a mermaid. She was absolutely lovely, with long flowing blond hair that covered her breasts like a cloak.

As we came up to her she smiled. I asked who she was. There were several butterflies floating above her head. She reached out her hand and one landed on the tip of her finger. Then she spoke, her voice was very soft, like a hushed whisper. But I had no difficulty hearing her because even though her voice was soft, it was filled with power.

"You have journeyed far?" she asked.

"Yes," I said.

"What has brought you and your friend here?"

I told her about my Island, the animals and about the large Black Bird who dropped the Rose.

She said that the one I seek is called the Great Falcon of the Golden Perch and that for me to find him I would have to travel through the mist of confusion.

"What is that?" I asked her.

"A place from which there are many ways in and only one way out!"

I didn't understand.

She only smiled and said, "Perhaps some day you will."

Then she pointed her hand at me and said, "Follow her, she will guide you." And the butterfly flew from her finger and she, the Lady of the Rocks, was gone.

Whale and I traveled on and on, following the butterfly. The Sun set into the water like a giant ball of fire. The butterfly glowed in the darkness of the night and we followed her like a beam, feeling tired and somewhat anxious, as we sailed on throughout the night.

When the sun came bringing light, I could see a wall of gray fog ahead of us which gave me a bad feeling. I could sense danger in there and did not want to enter. I told Whale to stop. The butterfly hung in the air for a few moments then flew towards me. It hovered just above my head and then it flew away towards the fog.

Whale said, "This must be the mist the Lady of the Rocks told you about."

"I know but I don't want to go in there," I said.

"What else can we do?" he asked. "The Lady of the Rocks sent us the butterfly to guide us. I think we'll be alright."

And so we went into the fog. Soon we lost sight of the butterfly and I told Whale to turn back. I panicked and wanted to get out but no matter which way we went we could not get free. Then I remembered what she had said, that there were many ways in but only one way out. So we sat in the water and waited until we got a glimpse of the butterfly. Its tiny body giving off light and we followed it deeper and deeper into the mist. Many times I wanted to pull away and break free of this terrible fog that surrounded me. Sometimes I would see that in one direction the mist seemed lighter and think "There, that's the way out," and I'd get angry and filled with mistrust because this butterfly ignored this and instead took us deeper into the darkness and the thickness of the mist. Taking me further and further into a place I did not want to go.

Why should I trust this butterfly? For that matter why should I trust the whale? At one point when we passed what appeared to be the way out I thought of sliding off Whale's back without him knowng and swimming toward the lightness. But something inside me held me back and I thought that come what may I'd see this through and trust the butterfly. As soon as I'd made that decision the fog vanished, the mist was gone and Whale, Butterfly and I were in the light.

Butterfly turned toward me and her message came
into my mind though she did not speak. "Trust." And then
she was gone.

We could see a large shape ahead and Whale and I
followed. As we got closer we could see that ahead of us
was a mountain range that stretched across the ocean like
a wall or a dam. But there was a narrow passageway
through the mountains and we headed straight for it.

When we were about a mile away I saw something
just beyond the pass. There was a huge golden tree that
must have been three miles high.

As we were about to enter the pass the water ahead
began to bubble and swirl and suddenly a huge three-
headed dragon came up and blocked the passageway
through the mountains. It was hideous and vulgar and
snapped its jaws at us and bared its foul brown teeth.

"Run, Whale!" I screamed, and he pulled us back
and away. We cut through the water at great speed until I
realized that the monster wasn't chasing us, that it was
holding its position guarding the pass.

Then I saw something out of the sky. It was Lion.
He landed on a rock sticking out of the water a short
distance away from us. Whale and I were very glad to see
him and as we sailed over to the rock I now saw that he
was not alone. Above and behind him sat the Lady of the
Rocks and there were three butterflies fluttering and hovering just above her head.

Lion gave me his old familiar smile and the Lady of

the Rocks said, "You have reached the end of your journey, for there is the perch of the Great Falcon. Why do you sit out here in the water?"

"Because of the monster. It's hideous and it blocks the path."

"I see," she said.

Then she reached into the water and pulled out a sword and held it out to me.

And she said, "With this you must face the beast."

Then she stretched out her hands and the three butterflies flew straight up into the air and came together. They joined and began to spin around and around growing into a large ball of colors. The faster they spun the larger the ball became, like a multicolored top spinning wildly. The sky grew dark and lightning flashed across the sky. Suddenly the ball exploded and there appeared a winged battle horse, a great winged white stallion. I climbed into the saddle and felt the power of this magnificant animal underneath me.

"You have the power to slay the monster," the Lady said.

"Lion will you come with me?"

"I shall watch from here," he said.

I pulled up on the reins and the horse flew up and then headed straight for the pass. When we arrived the monster cringed before us in fear, but it would not let us pass.

"I can destroy you now," I said.

It looked at me, all three faces, the left sided head was angry and snarling and baring its yellow stained teeth, the right sided head was grinning at me, mocking me, laughing at me. The head in the center was silent but from it I sensed fear and thought that I saw tears in its eyes.

The monster backed up onto the shore and finally stopped with its back against the golden tree. I raised my hand to kill it but I couldn't, instead I tossed the sword into the sea and dismounted the great white battle horse and it flew away. As I looked at the monster I now knew that I was looking at a part of myself. Fear, anger, and meanness, suspicion, arrogance, and guilt. The monster began to decrease in size, like a balloon with a leak, until it was no bigger than I was.

It was still frightening to look at, misshapen and ugly. I knew that I had to touch it. I walked to it. It shook with fear and distrust. The left head snapped at me with it's jaws and the right head called me names. I could not turn away. I reached my hand out and with the tip of my finger I brushed away a tear from the eye of the center face, and then all three cried out in such pain that I could only put my arms around it and hold it tightly. And I knew that this was not a monster, it was a baby, a tiny, helpless child who had been torn apart by violence, abuse, and neglect, by those who were supposed to love and care for him.

I drifted off to sleep and when I awoke, Lion was beside me.

"Where is the dragon?" I asked.

"Where it has always been," he answereed.

"Inside of me?" I asked.

He smiled, and that was all that he needed to do.

I looked about for Whale, but did not see him, and I was concerned because he and I had become very close on this trip.

Reading my thoughts Lion said, "The Lady of the Rocks sent Whale home. He was very tired from the quest. And she also left a gift for you."

From behind Lion's wing a beautiful butterfly flew up and landed on the tip of my nose. Both Lion and I laughed.

Then he said, "The Lady of the Rocks told me to say that this little butterfly will always know where to find her should you need her advice again."

I was very pleased by her kindness to me and happy to welcome butterfly into our family.

I looked upwards at the giant golden tree. It stretched into the sky like a huge building.

Lion said, "Are you ready?"

I nodded my head, yes, then I climbed on top of his back, with butterfly resting in the palm of my hand, and we flew upwards higher and higher and landed at the very top of the tremendous golden tree. The three of us stood before the Great Falcon of the Golden Perch. He was great in size, huge. His hard, piercing black eyes looked right into my soul. I knew there was nothing this magnificent beast did not know about me. So no explanation was nec-

essary.

> *For a long time we stood in total silence.*
>
> *Finally, the Great Falcon spoke, "Behold!"*
>
> *And there at my feet was the Rose.*
>
> *I reached down, put my hands on the stem, and I tried to pick up the Rose but it was still too heavy.*
>
> *The Great Falcon said, "The Rose is Love. It's beauty represents the joy and pleasure of love. The weight represents the pain and responsibility of love."*
>
> *With that he stretched out his giant wings and flew up and away.*
>
> *Lion was at my side. He said, "We will stay here for awhile, and you will speak again to the Great Falcon. But now it is time for you to rest and think about what he has said to you."*
>
> *As always, Lion was right. I was tired, and I felt myself drifting of to sleep.*

The changes that Joe underwent during his work with Margaret involved a recovery of his self esteem, the development of a deep and natural compassion, and the ability to feel and to once again trust his feelings. His imagery expresses not only the classical themes of mythology and their spontaneous generation within Joe, but also the uniqueness of his personal journey.

We can see the beautiful interweaving of the universal and the personal in this journey of self discovery. It is the story of an injured man finding his natural relationship to the universe, returning to wholeness along his journey.

Science and Shamanism

The realm of science has developed out of the conjunction of two of the modes of knowing: sensing and thinking.

The "scientific method" fundamentally involves making a prediction from a theory and then going into the laboratory or the field and manipulating a single variable with the intention of proving or disproving the prediction. The scientist then returns to the theory with these results, incorporates them into the theory, and makes derivations from this theory, predicting new results that can be verified through further (sensory) observation. This process takes place in a situation where all variables are controlled as much as possible and where the events can be measured. Ultimately, the scientist arrives at a point where events can be predicted and therefore controlled by stipulating and controlling their antecedents.

This continued movement back and forth between objective (sensory) observation and intellectual theorizing has provided us with a tightly woven description of a manner in which the sensed dimension functions. In particular, the emergence of the fact that changes in certain aspects of the sensed world coincide with aspects of a specialized way of thinking (mathematics), has led directly to our ability to create tools and manipulate our existence in the world with an unprecedented degree of control.

The very success of science has made it difficult for us to see its shortcomings. The most serious shortcoming is its propensity to subordinate the two other modes of knowing, i.e., feeling and imagery, to fit within its tenets. We have become so fascinated with the predictability and control that science has given us over the dimensions of thinking and sensing that we think the descriptions derived from them must also hold true for feeling and imagery.

But we must realize that each window of knowing is unique; each provides us with dimensions of experience that cannot be reduced to any of the other three. And even if we employ some equivalency, such as counting the number of heartbeats, it is vital that we recognize fully that the counting is never the heartbeat itself. It is only through the balanced and harmonized *experience* of all four windows, each valued for what it itself is, that we can come into our true being.

Thus science, in the nonintelligent way we have grasped it as a belief system that excludes, has come to be a primary detractor from the possibility of our movement into Being.

Let me emphasize that science itself is not at fault. The problem lies in the all-too-human way we insist on holding it as a conceptual territory within which we seek the comfort of security (see next chapter). It has become the haven within which we think our control will provide safety and survival.

Whereas thinking and sensing are the scientist's primary modes of knowing, feeling and imagery are the primary modes by means of which the shaman knows. He recognizes imagery as foundational, preceding and transcending knowing through thinking and sensing, although definitely overlapping with those modes. He knows feeling as the energy of aliveness and as a means of perception. To enter the dimension in which he is effective, he shifts his attention to the windows of feeling and imagery. Interacting with another being, he can touch their deep imagery and energy in such a way that it begins to help them move toward greater wholeness, toward greater health.

To the scientist such an orientation may sound magical or mythical, that is, not logical. And this is true: logic is a facet within the window of thinking, and imagery and feeling are experiential dimensions. The scientist may be quick to make judgments and evaluations about imagery and feeling, even though he has typically refrained from exploring these dimensions directly, sitting instead on the sidelines trying to understand them by looking through the window of thinking.

Thinking *about* imagery, and thinking *about* feeling, can tell us much about the structure of thinking, how it would arrange the *concepts* that it can derive from feeling and imagery, but it is perhaps poetry, music, and art that come closest to representing feeling and imagery at the cultural level. Allowing oneself to plunge headlong into imagery and feeling is a journey in itself.

Of course the shaman must have first come to his own fullness in the dimensions of imagery and feeling to be capable of navigating this terrain. Characteristically the shaman is first "chosen" in some way. Perhaps through a dream, he is "sent" an experience that communicates the fact that imagery and feeling will be major windows in which he will live. He is then stripped of his identification with the body as object, characteristically his flesh is removed and his bones are washed clean, or perhaps he is devoured by an animal. He comes to a new way of knowing who he is, not as an objectified physical body, but through the full windows of imagery and feeling. The body that is purely felt is invisible, centered at the heart of the universe and aware of the universal energy. For feeling there is no dividing line between energies: all energy is one. And imagery has become the foundation of his seeing.

Westerners, and particularly scientists, have long had difficulty with shamans because they try to force the shaman into the windows of thinking and sensing, where the scientist is thoroughly ensconced but where the shaman will not fit. Few scientists have been willing to journey to the dimension where the shaman lives. The journey is necessarily an experiential one, entailing meetings with awesome and sometimes terrifying creatures. Scientists tend to equate the window of imagery, where the shaman journeys, with the window of sensing, because the same language is used in describing both, or else to diminish the validity and importance of the shaman's journey and to consider it as not "real."

Westerners have removed themselves from the windows of feeling and imagery. They have built incredible institutions intent on wrenching each child away from those windows as well. The cruel manner in which Westerners sought to "educate" Native children, removing them from their parents, punishing them for using their own language, disallowing their relationship with nature, is but a mirror for the way each one of us has been wrenched away from our own at-homeness with the windows of feeling and imagery.

But we are at a time now where we can begin to appropriately employ the facts of imagery with precision in the manner in which they affect and enhance healing and health, growing and maturing, creativity and expression. Not as tools controlled from the thinking ego, for this is still a relationship of master and servant, but with imagery as a dimension fully the equal of thinking and respected as such.

The greater scientists have been open to knowing through all windows, even though the general social atmosphere at the time required that they pose their understanding in the format then palatable within the general belief system.

Jung was of course the giant among these, and knew that he could easily be ridiculed if he did not anchor his knowing of imagery within the scientific and academic custom of his time. He used his remarkable intellect to document prior occurrences of what he was being shown in imagery. He understood that the realm of historical alchemy dealt with an entry into the knowing of imagery, and the growth, healing, and transformation that were accessible through that window.

Einstein was completely at home in the window of imagery, and most of his insights came to him through that window. He rode on beams of light as if they were vehicles for travel, and saw the relationships that inhere within the bounds of light, space, and time.

August Kekule discovered the benzene ring by paying attention to his dreams, the form of the benzene ring appearing to him as a snake swallowing its tail. How many other chemists might not benefit from having access to the dimension of imagery, so that rather than waiting for the dream to bring the answer, they could voluntarily enter the window of imagery, asking of it what it knows of the problems they are researching.

Otto Loewi is said to have dreamed the experiment which provided for the discovery of chemical transmission at the synapse. In fact, he couldn't remember the dream the first night it occurred, although he knew it was important, so the dream came again on the following night, whereupon he arose immediately, went to his laboratory and verified the communication of the dream through a now classic experiment. And how many countless other scientists have followed a faint hunch that itself was only the faintest bit of feeling or imagery.

The window of imagery obviously wants us to know and understand this great universe and is willing to participate in its discovery. But how many scientists are trained in the use of imagery in their work? They are trained to make keen observations through the window of sensing, particularly when involved in measurement, that is, the evaluation of quantity through thinking. They are thoroughly trained to view through the window of thinking, particularly through that specialized facet of thinking called logical deduction. If they would also be trained in imagery they would have access to a tremendous and valuable resource which would amplify the possible directions they could look when devising experiments. The possiblity of seeing interrelationships when theorizing would be greatly expanded. Their own appreciation of the beauty of the universe and of being alive, the depth and complexity of their own human nature, would deepen and enrich their endeavors in an incalculable way.

The evolution in which we currently find ourselves is one of a change in concentration or focus rather than one requiring rejection of the old. It is a move toward the healthy inclusion of imagery and feeling in our lives as valid modes of knowing. There will be people for whom these modes are a natural path, just as there are now people who naturally gravitate toward thinking and/or sensing, because that is what they're good at. The new man will not be a scientist who rejects feeling and imagery, nor a shaman who rejects science, but a whole man who lives in the full complexity of his being.

Identity and Being

We must go deeper into the origins of the peculiar discordance in the relationship between the four windows of knowing than to simply attribute this discordance to the particular social customs and circumstances as I have done to this point.

For, although the way a child is treated undoubtedly serves to structure the environment in which survival is necessary, one must also ask both why the misalignment with the universe is so seemingly universal that people have to work continuously in order to stay aligned, and also why a human would reject dimensions of who he or she is? A significant aspect of the problem may lie specifically in who we are, in our identity.

The self, the ego, or one's identity, which are essentially different names for the same thing, arises out of a mistaken application of the dimensions of territoriality to the conceptual realm. Thus it is founded within the window of thinking. Our identity has its broadest anchor in the window of thinking. It is this anchor that particularly limits the extent of our exploration of the totality of our being.

The Territorial Self

When I first read Robert Ardrey's book *The Territorial Imperative* (1966) I was immediately struck by the similarity between the posturings used by an animal in warning intruders away from its territory and the ego defense mechanisms in Freudian personality theory. After further research I saw that the structure and use of an animal's territory and the human being's ego seem to have the same foundation.

Seemingly all animals establish a physical space in which they live or which is at least vital to the primary aspects of their living. Such a space has two principal dimensions: a center and a boundary.

The center is characteristically the place where feeding, sleeping, nurturing, love making and the bearing of young take place.

The boundary, the limiting edge of that space, is demarcated by specific objects that are readily recognized: stones, trees, bushes, fence posts, and things that are relatively easy to identify. These inform the animal whose territory it is exactly where its territory begins and ends, and thus whether the animal is inside or outside its territory. Some animals mark the boundary in specific ways: by urinating, defecating, or rubbing it with scents secreted by specific glands.

The boundary has two specific dimensions with respect to the male's stance and emotions: The inside of the boundary is a place of courage and aggression while the outside is a place of fear and retreat.

Typically, if the animal is inside his territory and another animal approaches, especially one that looks very similar to himself, he will perform a series of stereotyped postures or behaviors that warn the intruder away: the robin puffs out his red breast, the dog barks and bares his teeth, the bull snorts and paws the ground. These are all standard behaviors designed to warn the intruder away. If these postures do not result in withdrawal then the territory owner may physically attack the other.

If, however, the animal is outside the boundary of his own territory when he encounters another territory owner, his primary propensity is to flee back to his own territory.

Niko Tinbergen, in one of an interesting series of experiments with the three-spined stickleback (a small and highly territorial fish), captured two male sticklebacks who occupied adjacent territories in an aquarium and placed each one in a separate glass test tube filled with water. He then immersed the test tubes in the aquarium and moved them both back and forth from one territory to the other. The stickleback that was in its own territory would turn menacingly toward the other and the other would try to flee. Of course neither could go anywhere since they were confined in their individual test tubes. Tinbergen then moved them slowly across the tank. As soon as the territorial boundary was crossed their actions would reverse: the one that had been trying to flee now turned and tried to attack and the other tried to flee (Tinbergen, 1970).

There is an apparent advantage in fighting on one's own territory, for if a physical attack does occur, the animal who is fighting on his own territory characteristically wins, other things being relatively equal.

In the structure of a human identity we find such

similar dimensions and functions that I can only conclude that the substructure of identity is territoriality. However, in the human identity words and concepts have come to play a dominant role as bounding elements around a conceptual space. This is what I call a conceptual territory.

Go to any cocktail party and you see almost everyone engaged in posturing at a territorial boundary. People are emitting vocalizations that establish or indicate to the other their territorial boundaries. The vocalization of a specific name and the making of specific bodily movements: e.g., touching hands, curtsying, nodding, smiling are the initial behaviors in a territorial encounter. This is quicky followed by the vocalization of the boundaries of a more extensive territory: vocalizations indicating the place where one was born, where one lives, the kind of work one does, the schools one attended, subjects studied, etc., are all the displays of a territory *at the conceptual level*. We carry such a conceptual territory around with us all our lives, bringing aspects of it readily forth and displaying them whenever we meet another human. Such intense territorial marking is our fundamental obsession. It is an activity that so preoccupies us that it renders us unavailable to immediately experience our being. Our attention goes immediately to our conceptual territory and so is unavailable to our direct experience in the moment. Many people even when alone are constantly engaged in verbalizing their territories.

Now, it may be that an animal's space also serves as a kind of identity. It identifies the animal relative to a very specific piece of terrain and provides a surrounding space that is protective. As long as the animal protects his protective space, as long as he warns intruders away from his own space, or himself escapes from their territory *before* a physical encounter, he is less likely to come under direct physical attack and thus is more likely to survive. As long as the space around him is protected and defended, physical injury is less likely to occur. It also serves as a protective space for his mate and his young, for those *other being* aspects of himself.

It is also possible that thinking itself originated from the establishment of territories. After all, the territory is a kind of abstraction that is in fact *created* by the animal and his relationship to that terrain; it does not exist as a separate entity in itself. In treating that space as an entity the animal is in fact thinking, although not in words. It is true, however, that the animal's relationship to the territory is closely related to different kinds of vocalizations and expressive displays. Perhaps language as a coherently interrelated aggregation of sounds indicating a dimension other than the sounds themselves had a lengthy origin in the animal's need to announce and protect a territory.

The sudden effusion of *precise* sounds, i.e., the evolution of language itself, is a dimension that still engulfs the majority of mankind. If the origin and rapid differentiation of these sounds *is* within territoriality, then it would not be surprising to find that the function of language would be increasingly precise delineation of this spatial dimension, i.e., *to describe the boundaries of one's "reality" in greater and greater detail.* And the reality, of course, would be, at least initially, primarily physical, or that experienced through the sensing window.

Language, being the principal indicant of a human territorial boundary, would evolve in a much closer relation to sensing, rather than to feeling and imagery. Thinking would then tend to divide itself into the dimensions of safety and threat, or inside and outside of the territory. This may be the origin of the tendency to think in polarities. The ability to recognize the boundary of that space *within which one is safe* would be a principal function of sensing. Either at its limit or beyond, the realm of the identified boundary would be a place of constant alertness and potential threat.

Thus thinking and sensing would naturally be oriented outward, toward the outer boundary, for safety's sake, and it would almost seem foolhardy, as if one were abandoning one's defenses, to turn inward. The male, particularly, learns to patrol the boundary, moving along that line whose one surface is courage and attack, and whose other surface is fear and retreat. The female will join in this patrolling from time to time, but her place is closer to the center, toward the place of the origins of new life, nurturing and safety.

Furthermore, perhaps the male must have a female he can turn to in order to know where center is. She becomes an element within the territory that bespeaks warmth and nurturing. Yet he is constantly drawn back to that boundary with other males as both the threat and the proof of his courage.

Many boys are forced to assume an early identification with manhood. If the one characteristic of manhood, however hidden, is the establishment and defense of a conceptual territory, then there is no place to relax; the boy must be constantly alert and active, constantly churning out the territory. Thus his life becomes a continuous defense, a prolonged stereotyped posturing. The epitome (or one of them) would be the stereotyped posture of the military officer. (But then, most strong male identities would be stereotyped, almost caricatures.)

Thinking is the stereotyped posturing that is performed whenever the boundary of the conceptual territory is threatened. It is not just something we do from time to time but an obsessive and compulsive preoccupation. But it is also the activity that itself creates those identifiable concepts that delineate the boundary. Thus, the absence of thinking is itself the greatest threat to the conceptual territory, and this gives rise to a flurried activity of thinking to reestablish and defend that territory. When thinking endlessly perpetuates the illusion of an identity, then we can understand why the self would suddenly dissolve upon the cessation of thinking, as in a Zen satori, for example.

With the development of the *conceptual* territory in humans, boundaries, their protection and defense, have been the qualities accentuated by the male, whereas centeredness, generativity, and nurturing have been those of the female.

Sensing and thinking are the masculine qualities. They are masculine because they have been essential to the male guarding the boundary of the territory. Whereas feeling and imaging have been the qualities employed by the female whose domain is the center of the territory where food is prepared, sleep occurs, and the young are born and nurtured.

Yet because they became conceptual territories rather than physical territories they must be constantly manufactured in order to be real, i.e., one's attention must constantly be focused on the continued conceptualization and validation. The territory then becomes a characteristic of one's identity rather than just a place where one spends one's time. And the opposite becomes a place to be avoided!

The conceptual territory polarizes our awareness into two dimensions: those elements that are within the territorial boundary and those that are outside it. Or, in other words, our main concern is not only who we are but also who we are not.

However we describe ourselves, a counterpoint, or opposite is immediately called into play. If I describe myself as strong then I am also describing myself as not weak. If "strong" is an essential element in my conceptual territory then "weak" becomes my greatest threat. And I must constantly perform in a way that shows my strength and avoid performing in any way that indicates weakness. This is particularly true at the verbal level. If someone calls me weak I must go through all kinds of verbal posturings, and perhaps physical ones as well, in order to insure, at least myself, that I am not weak. The majority of time spent in our inner dialogues is taken up by arguments between these two dimensions.

An interesting excercise is to list all of the qualities of who you are and then describe yourself in the opposite terms and see how it feels. The feelings are tremendously intense. Why would a mere description create such intense feelings and lengthy ruminations?

It is also evident that if we take seriously the description of who we are (and it frequently becomes a powerful belief system) then the greatest threat is someone else who describes us in the opposite way. Our biggest threat is another verbal human being. And our greatest support is a human being who agrees with our description. So another verbal human is both the biggest threat and the greatest possible support. Thus must I align myself with similar thinking people and from this a culture is created.

In truth — and by truth I mean the best alignment that words can have with the way the universe works — this polarity is far too narrow for the rich complexity of our true being. So whatever the *description* of who we are, it is too confining; it is a limitation of our true dimensions.

The Buddhists say that there is a place where we are one with the universe, where all of the qualities of the universe are qualities of ourselves.

Social Boundaries

Human social ritual springs from the interface between territories and is intimately related to the expressive and defensive posturing that the animal engages in at the boundary of his territory. Humans display many extensions of this posturing depending upon the level of territory involved. Obsessive-compulsive activities of the neurotic are the expression of ritual at the boundary of the conceptual territory, when it is threatened by elements from the deeper self, particularly the emotional elements of anger or fear, but also perhaps elements of the realization of the falseness of their own identity.

The social rituals of politeness and manners are a ritual that characterizes the meeting of territories within the larger social configuration. In fact, ritualized activity at this level is sometimes the only social activity some people engage in: all of their social interaction is ritualized posturing; nothing is real or true or deeply felt. Some parents are quick to want to shove their children into this dimension, confusing it with authentic relationship. In fact, many people hunger for authentic relationship but find themselves trapped in the confines of an early learned social ritualizing. For example, they find themselves smiling when they know they are sad, or feel like crying, or are angry and afraid. The social territorial boundary ritual of smiling takes precedence over the experience that might be shared were they in the center of their territory with a trusted loved one. But frequently even the loved one is encountered in such a manner, i.e., *any other human being* is met as the territorial other.

Ceremony, on the other hand, is something deeper, even though it may be confused with ritual in people who have never truly experienced ceremony. In fact, we might say that ceremony is the ritualized doorway that leads us to

114

a relationship with our deeper, truer being. Ceremony is an activity deliberately engaged in (rather than automatically engaged in) that connects us to a deeper dimension of existence. Thus it is actually the opposite of social ritual, which takes us away from who we are into a stylized, generalized person.

We should also note that we have a natural propensity to engage in ritual at certain ages. Sometimes we have been forced to engage in it long before the critical age has arrived, and it then becomes a means of surviving criticism or avoiding punishment, i.e., an avoidance reaction rather than a positive engagement.

One may also ask, why, if our identity *is* formed from concepts that we ourselves continuously manufacture, we do not each then manufuacture sparkling identities to carry around. Why would a person maintain the identity of someone who fails, or of someone who is constantly miserable? We must remember that an identity is not formed in a vacuum. The childhood in which we learn to survive is filled with adults maintaining *their* territories. What happens to a child whose parent insists on owning all the strength in the family, or all the understanding? So that the only thing available to the other members of the family is to take on the polar quality as a way of maintaining the identity of the parent? Could this be why so many children must leave home before they can discover their true identities? Or why some children never dare?

The Shadow

Work with polarity animals involves going to each of the two poles of an energy continuum, inviting an animal to come forth out of each pole, getting to know them and their circumstances before bringing them together so they can interact, and doing what is necessary to move toward harmony. The ultimate possibility involves asking the two animals if they would be willing to merge together. There may be work that needs to happen with them individually before they are ready to merge, but when and if they do they usually transform into an animal that is different from either. At that time the individual also undergoes some changes.

An extension of this is the recognition that a person's identity is actually one pole on a continuum of the energy of Being: my identity is actually one end of a polarity. The other pole is what has sometimes been called the Shadow — an identity whose rejection helps maintain the identity one owns. So it is a serious encounter when one finally comes face to face with one's opposite pole and recognizes that the ultimate growing involves merging oneself with one's opposite.

In my own work this realization suddenly began coming to me as I was guiding a trainee through some difficult work during one of my training programs. I began to see a woman over my trainee's left shoulder. I recognized certain characteristics of this woman. They belonged to a woman I had known in Santa Fe who I did not care for at all: qualities of grasping, manipulation, a certain hardened cruelty, and a tremendous ego-centeredness. Not surprisingly, she was also a woman with whom I had a very difficult time relating. I wanted to escape from her and yet there was almost a compulsiveness about hearing her out and giving her whatever she was asking for. There were also other characteristics of the woman I was seeing over my trainee's left shoulder that did not belong to the Santa Fe woman, and I began to recognize that I was seeing my own opposite pole. I was fascinated by her and by what I was recognizing about myself.

I waited until the session with my trainee had ended and then told the group what had been occurring with me, that I had recognized for the first time that who we are is one pole of the energy of our being. It is the location within our being around which we have crystallized an identity, and being a pole it also has an opposite that helps maintain it, namely all those characteristics that we would reject most vociferously and whose exclusion maintains the one we call "me".

Manus Campbell, the only other man in the group, offered to guide me. I lay down on the floor with my arms open to the sides. As he guided me through the relaxation I found myself out in the countryside lying on a large marble funeral bier surrounded by many animals. Up in the sky at a comfortable distance but directly opposite me was the woman whose characteristics I have partially described to you, my opposite pole. I was aware that she was also relatively luminous. I asked the animals what needed to happen. They said that I was to merge with this woman. I felt sick at the thought and I also felt, particularly in my left side, a definite revulsion toward her. She began to move slowly toward me and as she did the revulsion became stronger. I became concerned almost to the point of panic. I asked the animals again if they were sure that merging was what needed to happen, and they all nodded as affirmatively as possible. So I just let myself feel whatever I was feeling as she came closer and closer. My breathing became very rapid and I noticed that it was centered in my solar plexus. As she came in contact with me, my body went into spasms and I could feel the air being completely forced out of my lungs. I was experiencing intense and strange emotions. I observed in wonder as she continued on through me and into the earth and I rose into the sky. As she entered the earth the marble funeral bier on which I had been lying closed over her like a door. I felt strange at this reversal of positions and had the faint sense of the earth as feminine and the sky as masculine and of me belonging more appropriately in the sky than on the earth. And yet the earth itself had been my grounding animal (or element) for many years, supporting me, nurturing me, providing me with a home wherever I happened to be. I felt a slight loss at what had just happened. I spoke to the earth and asked if she were still my grounding animal. The answer that came immediately from all around was, "The Universe is now your grounding animal!" I could feel myself held in the arms of the Universe, very gently, as if I were a young baby. It felt delicious. The Universe said to me, "I have always held you, and I always will." I felt the deep truth of this, and I also felt that the Universe truly holds each one of us and loves each one of us. I was also aware of how easily we lose sight of this fact.

As I returned to the room, I felt a beautifully close connection with each person in that room. I also felt a lightness about my body and moved with little effort. Since that time there has been something definitely different about me although it's quite difficult to articulate. I feel it now as I write this. My writing is almost effortless. I have no question about what I should say and what I shouldn't. The words just flow. In my work I feel a deeper connection with my clients and trainees. What I do and say with them comes more spontaneously and I feel a warm tenderness toward them. My voice seems to have a much wider degree of modulation. I feel richly energized and have no concerns about my appearance.

Knowing Oneself

There are two ways that we know the process of change: in its immediacy, i.e., as we observe it ongoing right now, and by comparing something present with what is stored in memory. When we meet someone who is now different than they were when we previously met them, it is because we have the memory of the previous meeting that we become aware of the fact that they have changed. Memory is essential for our knowledge of change occurring over long periods of time.

However, when we impose upon memory the demand that some previous element be recalled with consistency, memory becomes the agent of that which is static, it carries a pattern that is imposed as unchangeable. When we demand that greater truth be given to what is remembered than to what is immediately observed, we are creating a vital breach in our wholeness. Particularly in the memorization of that which is verbal do we become the purveyors of the unchanging pattern; in many instances we have mistaken this for education.

These two ways of knowing change are of the greatest significance when we try to know ourselves. I can know myself as the ongoing change that is occurring right now in this present moment. To do so requires that I be willing to experience myself fully and profoundly, to come into direct contact with my fundamental ongoing aliveness.

On the other hand, if I know myself in comparison to the memory of the past, then I constantly compare the present moment to the past. To do this the present moment must be continually reduced to words, to thinking: this divides me in two. The comparison entails a continuous ongoing judgment. We have already seen that the principal function of the window of thinking is labelling, comparing, and categorizing. So when our knowledge of who we are comes primarily through the window of thinking we are bound to exist in constant comparison and to feel continuously judged.

The frozen memory against which we constantly compare is a description of ourselves anchored in the memories of the events: things that happened to us, that we performed or achieved, or which were described to us by others along the route of coming to this present place in our lives. The "personal past" is a narrow band of description and memory to which we have given the designation "real" and to which we attribute the foundation of our present lives. This has become "who we are." But it is actually a dimension that freezes us in who we have been, that stultifies evolution, that restrains our fulfillment. It is the dimension that keeps us from becoming who it is we are destined to be in the fullness of our growing.

The energy and feelings that are knotted into this narrow band can be freed by ceasing the constant comparison and by allowing *ourselves* to merge back into all of the windows of knowing. In order for this to happen, however, we must sacrifice our identity, for identity is locked into that narrow band, is anchored in it. Identity is the frozen description of ourselves in comparison. Once the merging is complete, then who we are springs directly from the fullness of our personal mythology which is always a living event in the present. It springs directly from our feeling as an ongoing experience, from our immediate awareness of the surrounding circumstances of the present moment. We cease to find ourselves swallowed up in what thinking describes and instead recognize that who we are springs directly from an awareness of thinking as an ongoing process that we perform.

Thought in Control of Attention

Our minds have become filled with the continuous story we keep telling ourselves about who it is that we are. This is the primary structure of our conceptual territory. It seemingly keeps us contained within safe, already known boundaries and it keeps the rest of the world at bay, particularly the farther reaches of that world, which constitute the unknown and the feared.

But it also requires the participation of the world. For the story to continue to be true, we must control those aspects of the world that comprise our environment. The ongoing description of who we are most meaningfully emanates from the world around us. When it fails, however, we are quick to supply the missing elements. Who hasn't heard someone who has been deeply hurt talk to themselves about the event and put it in such a light that the hurt is either minimized or else retribution against the guilty party is imminent and forthcoming?

Thoughts are ways of guiding and steering attention so that who we are, and the world, continue along those lines that are already known and therefore safe. Thought does this by steering attention so that it is passed from one thought to another, continually, with no break. Thus even the thought of awareness leaving thinking and being oriented elsewhere is threatening, something to avoid. At this point, thought has captured attention and the inner commentary has become relentless.

The ultimate constant is awareness. But awareness gets concentrated into the spotlight of attention, and wherever attention is directed becomes our world. For an animal, awareness is full and fluid, that is, it goes where it goes and the animal follows. Since awareness is originally full, the animal has a center. Because of the extent of *our* evolutionary development we are capable of a tremendous awareness. But this Great Awareness becomes partitioned into numerous little attentions and pinned to a single spot no less than Gulliver was tied down and immobilized by the Lilliputians.

Within thinking, thought is capable of steering awareness in new directions. It allows us to anticipate the future and to reminisce about the past, to create new dimensions, theoretical worlds, science and science fiction. When we reach the point where attention is handed on from one thought to another and where thinking can no longer rest, thought has captured awareness. Since some thoughts feel more comfortable than others, thought steers awareness to those thoughts

aversion / clinging

that are comfortable and away from those that are not. Thus thought develops the capability of seeking out and avoiding. From this, thought develops the belief that if this kind of steering should cease to exist thought will lose control, will go crazy, will die. All of these consequences loom up as possiblilities and so thinking develops the belief that its continuity is essential to the survival of the organism. This, of course, is not true, but thought thrives on this belief for its own self-perpetuation. At this point thought begins to employ the deeper survival mechanisms for its own perpetuation. This reaction in itself eventually becomes detrimental to the survival and welfare of the organism.

As I have discussed already, our identity is taken from this continuity of thinking, this ongoing belief system that has captured attention. Once attention has been captured it is difficult for it to flow back into awareness. Meditation developed as a technique for bringing thought to the place where it will release attention from its grasp and allow awareness once again to flow freely. This may feel like the death of the individual, but it is actually the freeing of awareness from the grasp of thought and the allowing of the *belief system* of who we are to come to an end.

Imagery has described the capture of awareness in the myth of Prometheus, who stole fire from the Gods. As punishment he was nailed to a cliff where each day his liver was eaten out by birds and during the night it grew back again. This we essentially do to ourselves, pinning who we are to one limited identity that is maintained during the day by continuous thinking. During the night we once again allow a return to imagery, where the identity is seen in a fuller perspective relative to the rest of who we are. Dreams come from the larger beyond of who we truly are.

Sometimes this identity is just too much at odds with the circumstances of our lives; for example, the identity may be in direct opposition to the facts of our lives. A weak person may hold the belief that he is strong, or a strong person hold the belief that he is weak. The circumstances of one's life may reach such a peak that the identity crystallizes in opposition to the circumstances for awhile but eventually has to give way. If it gives way abruptly the change is termed a "psychotic break." Just before the rupture the obsession of trying to contain oneself within thinking reaches its most intense point.

It is possible for one to be freed from the identity gradually and easily, which is in essence what most religions were originally about. When they succeed they bring one into a sate of fluidity: of knowing oneself as continuous with the universe, not separated off from it but in ongoing relationship, participant with that larger Being that we are.

The difficulty is that many religions also become encrusted in belief systems that are reiterated and maintained with the same tenacity that pertains to most identities. In other words, the belief system of the religion becomes the structure of one's identity. It is at this juncture that religions fail the individual. It is also at this point that religions collide with one another.

persona

Identity always embodies a constraint of the totality of who one is. An identity is always a limitation. An identity always involves exclusion, separating oneseslf off from one's continuity with the Universe.

All of this brings up the question of who it is that is meeting with and interacting with the animals in deep imagery. Sometimes there is the experience of being directly present with the animals. At other times one can see an image of oneself in interaction with them, and this image of oneself has the potential to change, to become a child, or older than we actually are, or to have different appearances. The being who encounters the animals is one's identity, and imagery shows us that we have many identities. These are led by the animals through a series of experiences that result in a growth of the identities, frequently a merging of one into another, then an expansion, and ultimately a freeing.

The Drop Returns to the Sea

... "[A]ll the "outer" aspects [have been] accidental. Only what is interior has proved to have substance and a determining value. As a result, all memory of outer events has faded, and perhaps these "outer" experiences were never so very essential anyhow, or were so only in that they coincided with phases of my inner development."[12]

In this manner Carl Jung discusses his autobiography. What are we to understand by it? That Jung, with his phenomenal intellect, is just a bit sketchy when it comes to the

---

[12] G. Wehr. *Jung: A Biography*, Shambhala, 1988, p. 3.

memory of the specifics of his life? The truth is much deeper. Entry into deep imagery, or in his words into the unconscious, opens one's being in such a way that the events of one's life lose the connecting structure, the capacity for forming one's identity, that they have for the general population. The events of one's personal history melt into that much larger sea of the dynamics of one's deep imagery. The remembered events of one's past, are, after all, but small bits of imagery themselves. To hold them separate and structure an identity in terms of them is to divorce an energy that should be whole from its wholeness. Delving deeply into one's depths causes the boundaries of the identity that is sustained by the events of one's personal history to melt back into that sea of the deeper dynamics of one's Being. This outcome naturally ensues from entering into a dialogue with one's unconscious. This is the organic result of developing a respectful relationship with one's deep imagery.

The Time of Crippled Thinking

The Emotional Dark Ages

The Dark Ages was a period of time from 476 A.D. to 1000 A.D. when learning in Europe came to a standstill, and what had been previously learned was preserved in a few monasteries. Thinking ceased to explore new ground and became the rote repetition of standard lore. We emerged from that period of time, eventually into the Age of Reason, into the burgeoning world of creativity and invention in which we now live.

As a culture we are just now emerging from the *emotional* dark ages. We are emerging from a time when feelings were to be performed (or suppressed) by rote, without individual attention, style, uniqueness, without the freedom to explore that dimension, that window, as a way of knowing the universe. And the same is true for imagery. The imagery that was allowed has been a standard imagery, an imagery having to do with the origins of one's nation or one's family, and with one's relationship to the universe, to God. Not a freedom to explore one's own imagery, as it presents itself, as one discovers it to be, uniquely individual, but an imagery that was standardized and approved, an imagery that was dictated and dominated by thinking and control.

Let us hope that the opening of the windows of imagery and feeling will be as fruitful and as freeing of our natural humanness as opening the window of thinking was for our natural creativity and invention. In fact it will probably be more so, because it will also entail our coming into balance, where our four windows will all be open, and so our center will be true, and we, for the first time as a living organism, will enter into our true fullness and aliveness.

The Time of Crippled Thinking

I envision a time, perhaps as soon as a hundred years into the future, perhaps five hundred, when humans will be able to look back upon our own time and seriously wonder why it was we insisted on injuring our young and on perpetuating our own injuries.

Perhaps the nucleus of the injury will be viewed as having happened with René Descartes, who searched for some solid ground on which to base his existence, and arrived at the conclusion that *thinking* was that solid ground. Of course, he arrived at this conclusion through thinking about it, so we must be aware that thinking is coming up with a justification for its own existence. How can we blame it? If we seriously consider that thinking itself is speaking, or a person whose *identity* is lodged firmly in thinking, then the classic phrase, *I think, therefore I am* is the conclusion that the territorial identity arrives at, not the conclusion from wholeness. And we must admit that it is correct. *It is true of our identity but not of our being.* It is hoped that our descendants will look back on the injury caused by this approach and recognize that it stemmed from a misdrawn conclusion that thinking is the foundation of being.

129

It is from this conclusion that we justify the way we try to fill our children with thoughts and to shape them, condition them, and train them to fit our own demands and expectations. Otherwise we would be able to see that we are injuring them severely, that we are restricting their thinking from being the broad and global process that it was originally intended to be, instead turning it into a petty, rigid, limited fraction of its original self. This limited thinking has the primary function of justifying the child's existence to others, primarily parents and teachers.

Our future descendants, looking back at us, will ask the question, "How could they have been so blind?" Will they see that we were each trapped in a restricted conceptual territory, and that to justify that entrapment we then insisted on trapping each of our children as well?

We need to be birthed from the womb of thinking. We need to take the step of discovering a willingness to move forth into the unknown of ourselves. We must leave our firm ensconcement in the supposedly safe confines of thinking, where we must think everything through, have an answer for everything before we act, know before we allow ourselves the thrill of being.

Thinking is not the problem, the way we use thinking is. Or, it would be more proper to say, it is the thinking perspective from which we view ourselves and the world that is the problem.

As I have said, the problem is not with the thinking; the problem is that we are unaware of the thinking, and we think that our thoughts are true. They are not; they are only thoughts.

Thoughts are very similar to feelings in that they are invisible and thus it is easy to either discount them completely or attribute them to something or someone else. It is surprisingly easy to attribute thoughts to their referent, that is, to think that the thought *is* what the thought is about, that the thought itself is the same as the thing thought of. A thought is always a limitation of the thing thought; in particular, it omits the mystery of the thing.

Crushing a child's spirit begins early and with the best of intentions. Furthermore, it begins in a place where the parents are already fully unaware: with control by speech.

Who has not seen a young child bombarded by commands from parents to perform some sound, some gesture, some behavior, for the admiring others or as a convenience to the parent. "Smile for grandma." "Say goo goo." "Wave bye bye." "Close your eyes and go to sleep now." "Eat your food." "Go potty like a good little boy." "Stop crying." Absolutely no concern is given to the child's experience, whether the child is predisposed to do such a thing, or even whether it is in the child's best interests.

My wife and I have never required that our daughter eat what she is not disposed to eat, so there are times when she eats very little at a meal. But we have noticed that there are times that she absolutely devours whatever is put before her, and that these periods of devouring come in cycles. Furthermore, each period of devouring precedes a period of sudden growth. Something within the child anticipates when a period of growth is going to occur and ensures that she consumes the appropriate food and takes in the energy that will be needed for that growth. I often think that if we were the kind of parents that demanded she eat whatever was put on her plate, and if she in fact did this, that it would override that subtle mechanism that actually knows what she needs, and this fine tuning of her appetite in relation to the needs of her body would be demolished. She would then be eating for some other reason: to avoid our wrath, to not feel rejected, to appear as a good little girl, acceptable and lovable, and so forth. The fact is that she is a child that is deeply attuned to her needs and we have not sought to override her attunement with our own program. One can compare this child's experience with that of children who are fed on schedule from the time they are infants: their own needs, their own knowing, is sacrificed to the clock, that great invention of ours that has taken the subtleness and fluidity of change and packaged it into convenient chunks that can only be verified by the outer.

The sacrifice of our own inner knowing to the words or structure of someone else is the begining of the loss of spirit. Certainly there needs to be coordination: the activities of the parents must be coordinated with the needs of the child and for this some awareness on the part of the parents is required. But if the parent's own inner knowing has been overridden, if their awareness of themselves is gone, how can they possibly be attentive to that same element in a child?

So this is a problem that is perpetuated generation after generation. The way a newborn infant is treated in many hospitals, to say nothing of the way the mother is treated, is worse than a sin. A nurse actually said to me in preparation for drawing blood from my infant daughter's heel before she was even six hours old, "They don't feel anything at this age, they're not conscious." If she was not conscious and didn't feel, she would not have cried! She may not have a memory of the event that can be articulated but that is not the same as not being conscious! The sin is that we pass off ignorance for knowing, as this nurse did, and the place it begins is when our own inner knowing is overridden at a very early age.

Once I have abandoned the awareness of my own bodily state, what we could call my inner feelings, and attend instead to the words of someone else, I have given away responsibility for myself to the other. This is the beginning of war! War can only happen when people follow the demands of another, to invade, to kill, to overrun, rather than listening to their own deep feelings and inner voice. An army can never happen until we have made this breech.

Once we have given our awareness over to control by the words of the other, rather than allowing it to remain attuned to deep inner feelings, we are also beginning the divorce from ourselves. Then *our own* words will tend to override the inner knowing. This leads to a time when thinking becomes the despot, when thinking takes control and comes to fear or to think it must contain feeling. It is the period we have been in for the past four or five hundred years, and something we have been dancing with for the past five thousand. It is *not* a period of harmonious interrelation between the various aspects of who we are.

I call this a time of crippled thinking, because thinking, in order to be whole and sane must be in harmonious balance with the other aspects of who we are. But thinking has not been in such a position. We have all been trained to act as if thinking were supposed to be the dominant factor in our makeup. Thinking has been trained to feel that it needs to come up with an immediate answer, an immediate solution, to anything that happens in our lives. We have made of it a mechanical element, supposedly along the lines of reason and rationality, but ultimately along the lines of a machine, rather than allowing it to be the organic and alive process that it is. We have crippled thinking in the same way that the chief of the beggars every night puts a metal clamp on the leg of a child he has purchased in order for it to become crippled and therefore be a more profitable beggar. But our crippling, our clamp, has been applied during the day.

If we ever do become a balanced culture, a balanced world, our descendants will look back upon this period as one of singular insanity, a time when thinking overrode the depths of our remarkable humanity.

Obviously, what I am writing will be encountered first by thinking in anyone who reads it, so I am in fact addressing thinking at that place where it still remembers being in balance, or where our wholeness is still intact. For in us not only is thinking out of balance with the rest of our component aspects, but there is also the awareness that things are not right. Balance knows itself and is always available potentially as something to come back into, just as health knows itself and there is a recognition when we are not healthy, however subtle. Awareness of the imbalance is itself the beginning of a return to balance. Thinking itself knows when it is not at home in who we are. But it initially tends to blame the rest of who we are, rather than examining itself. *Know Thyself*, the words carved over the entryway of the Oracle at Delphi express an ancient understanding of wholeness: be aware of yourself, experience yourself, feel yourself, become friends with your imagery and feelings, let your thinking come back into its appropriate balance.

Language and Social Unification

In all of this rebalancing of the four windows let's not lose sight of the ultimate function of thinking and language, which is to unify us as human beings into a global organism. The component parts, i.e., individual societies, have been being whittled out for seven or eight thousand years now, fighting each other for survival, struggling, competing, but also complementing, discovering interdependency, and now, having explored all of those rough edges, ready for the final interlocking union, the ultimate integration into a single society of humans.

What is essential in all this is that we recognize the larger picture and that we acknowledge that *some* properties or dispositions of thinking and language lend themselves to deleterious outcomes.

Thus, rigid identification with a thought pattern is detrimental; recognition of the experience from which our Being springs is essential. One of the universal languages now available is the deep language of the experiences of the animals as allies and resources in our individual evolution and ultimately in our global interconnecting.

I have felt sometimes that this period from which we are just now emerging, this period of concentrated thinking and focus on science, has truly been a period of sacrifice. We have sacrificed our wholeness for a period of time in order to devise and establish those mechanisms and structures that have only recently begun to allow us almost complete and instantaneous communication with just about anyone else on this earth. The electronic fabric that now weaves human beings together was essential for the next step in our human evolution: the movement into becoming a responsible global organism.

The Ultimate Core of Our Aliveness

Several years ago I was guiding a friend to visit her inner animals. The session was deeply involved and intricate. It had gone on for over three hours. She had met a great wooly mammoth as her grounding animal and had journeyed within it to the position of one of its ovaries. There she was undergoing an experience that involved her own qualities of procreation when I suddenly began having a spontaneous experience. I found myself aware of the four billion years of my own evolution and I was sitting deeply in the center of it. From this position I was viewing the present moment. The place from which I was viewing was tremendously profound, and I saw my present life in relation to that center. There was not much to be overly concerned with. There was no need to identify with any particular culture. Culture was just one way of performing our aliveness. I was not at all concerned with how I might look to someone else: I could just as easily be a hunchback and it would not have mattered. There was not the least experience of any competitiveness. In fact it did not matter *who* I was. The experience was the experience of us all. I felt a tremendous kinship with all forms of life. I also felt a deep wish to help all people who had divorced themselves from these same roots to reconnect with them. I was aware of how lost and lonely people were in disconnection from this experience of their evolution, of their own rootedness.

We must recognize that this core of who we are is tremendously potent and profoundly alive. No belief about it is necessary. Beliefs are only functional at the surface, at the point from which we take a perspective and view things from a certain position. If the theory is in fact true, then the belief itself is not necessary. Getting in touch with the core and experiencing it is what is important, not the holding of a particular belief. The animals give us a powerful mode for interfacing with this core within ourselves and they lead us closer and closer to being in harmony with it. So actually no belief is necessary.

Perhaps it is possible to hold beliefs that in fact conflict with ultimate experience. Wouldn't it then be better to be without beliefs at all than to hold to those which interfere with our contact with the Ultimate. It is obvious that we cannot change the Ultimate by means of our beliefs. What we do change is our relationship to that Ultimate. Belief is actually a belief of who we are, of our relationship to the universe.

So my orientation is not one of beliefs or holding to them, but it is that certain beliefs can possibly interfere with our experience. The important thing is the experience itself. It is this experience that the animals are capable of leading us back to. Coming into the experience that is the energy of our most profound core of aliveness is what is important. So I am not putting forth a theory. I am inviting people to explore for themselves and see what the results are for themselves.

The ultimate understanding is that I am the energy myself. And all that I have been put through has shaped and sometimes deformed that energy. Can we allow ourselves to come back to that original energy and let go of those shapes into which we have been molded, the shapes that in fact keep us from being in contact with that energy? We mistake ourselves for the imposed shape when in fact it is the problem. It is what keeps us stuck to the surface. I am the problem to the extent that I believe myself to be in control of this energy core. The only control we could have over it would be to diminish and restrain ourselves in relation to it. In doing that the ego comes into existence.

Any belief system is a rigidification of orientation. And any belief being more important than experience is a detraction from the experience of this profound energy core.

My task is to align my aliveness with the aliveness of the Universe.

Maturity

Who we are as adults has unfortunately been structured by our beliefs *about* what it is to be an adult! The structure of adulthood has been formed by an immature individual speculating about adulthood and then trying to fill out that structure. The "maturity" of our culture is actually an immaturity maintained by the power of control and thus housed in the window of thinking.

True maturity evolves from the encounter with the totality of who we are and losing the battle, allowing who we have been to melt into the experience of the totality of who we truly are. This involves standing in the center of all four windows, trusting them all equally, recognizing that each is essential to a knowing of the universe and of ourselves. Knowing that who we are *and* the universe can never be fixed once and for all, is in a constant process of evolving, and is bathed in the mystery of its origin and its destination — yet it continues to evolve.

Knowing this, we cannot then force maturity on our children by stipulating the direction into which they must thrust their lives in order to grow. We can only, intelligently, nurture their growth into their own fullness and trust who it is who is emerging — and exult in that emergence.

Bibliography

Ardrey, Robert. *The Territorial Imperative: A Personal Inquiry into the Animal Origins of Property and Nations.* New York: Atheneum, 1966.

Bierhorst, John. *The Mythology of North America.* New York: William Morrow, 1985.

Gallegos, E. S. *The Personal Totem Pole: Animal Imagery, the Chakras, and Psychotherapy.* Santa Fe: Moon Bear Press, 1987, second edition 1990.

Jung, C. G. *Psychological Types.* vol. 6 of The Collected Works of C. G. Jung. Princeton University Press, 1921.

Tinbergen, N. *Fighting.* Chapter 4 of *Animal Aggression* edited by Charles H. Southwick, New York :Van Nostrand Reinhold Co., 1970.

Turner, Frederick. *Beyond Geography: The Western Spirit Against the Wilderness.* New Jersey: Rutgers University Press, 1983.

Vasington, Margaret. *Joe's Journey: One man's Heroic Search for his Soul* (currently in preparation).

Wehr, G. *Jung: A Biography.* Berkeley: Shamhala, 1988.

INDEX

About the Author

Steve Gallegos considers himself first and foremost a craftsman. He has worked in leather, wood, silver, stained glass, antique furniture restoration, painting, and most recently has been carving fossilized walrus teeth and painting Russian icons. He is certain that had he not been required to attend school he would today be a deeply contented and illiterate craftsman. Such is life.

He was born in 1934 to Eligio Gallegos and Katherine Powers Gallegos in the small village of Los Lunas, New Mexico, where he attended school and longed for summer vacation. During a sojourn in the Air Force he travelled around Europe as often as he could and began reading, discovering learning as opposed to schooling. He subsequently obtained degrees in psychology from the University of Wisconsin, New Mexico State University, and Florida State University. He spent many years as a Professor of Psychology, and served as Chairman of the Department of Psychology at Mercer University. His first act as Chairman was to make the position a rotating one with a one year tenure. The Dean insisted that it be a three year tenure.

He currently spends his time training therapists and others in the use of animal imagery, presenting workshops, and writing. He is a co-founder of Returning to Earth Institute, a program that guides people into the wilderness on vision quests and helps them return to the experiential ground of their being. He is also president and co-founder of the Institute for Visualization Research located in Embudo, New Mexico, a non-profit institute dedicated to education and research in the field of mental imagery.

He has recently completed a novel: *Little Ed and Golden Bear*, to be published soon by Moon Bear Press.

Other Books from Moon Bear Press

Moon Bear Press is a publisher of quality paperbacks concerned with psychotherapy, imagery, the inner quest, healing and growing into wholeness.

Our publications to date include:

The Personal Totem Pole: Animal Imagery, the Chakras, and Psychotherapy, Second Edition, by Eligio Stephen Gallegos, PhD. This book details the discovery and remarkable effect of the Chakra Power Animals in growth and healing. It retails for 12.00. (ISBN 0-944164-08-0)

Sacred Mountain: Encounters with the Vietnam Beast by Edward Tick, PhD. A deeply healing book about the therapist, a Vietnam war resister, and his personal experiences conducting therapy with Vietnam veterans. It retails for 9.95. (ISBN 0-944164-00-5)

A Queen's Quest: Pilgrimage for Individuation by Edith Wallace, MD, PhD. Dr. Wallace studied with Carl Jung in Switzerland and J. G. Bennett in England. She is a psychotherapist and leads workshops in the use of creative collage in exploring one's deeper self, which is the subject of this book. About 60 pages including 18 color plates. 8 1/2 by 11 inch format. It retails for 16.00. (ISBN 0-944164-21-8)

Being Space by Patrick de Sercey. A former Chairman of the Department of Philosophy at Valdosta State College, highly regarded for his teaching and now a psychotherapist, Patrick de Sercey presents an overview of our present social situation from the integrative perspectives of Existentialism, Buddhism, and Shaivism. 312 Pages, it retails for 14.00. (ISBN 0-944164-14-5)

Little Ed and Golden Bear by E. S. Gallegos. A moving novel about the education of Little Ed. The educational system of the future which will allow children to go on a two year adventure at the time of puberty. Little Ed journeys to the Northwest Coast to apprentice with a totem pole carver named Golden Bear. Here he is introduced to his inner animals. 150 pages. 10.00. (ISBN 0-944164-12-9) Available in 1992.

The Circus Cage: A Metaphoric Journey of Personal Growth by Rosalie G. Douglas. Available in 1992.

Meetings with Remarkable Animals edited by E. S. Gallegos. Available in 1992.

All of the above books are paperbacks.

These books may be ordered directly from Moon Bear Press, Box 15811, Santa Fe, NM 87506. Please include $2.00 postage and handling.